THE
BOOK
OF
MYSTERIES

Prayer Journal

THE
BOOK
OF
MYSTERIES

Prayer Journal

JONATHAN CAHN

FRONT
LINE

Most Charisma House Book Group products are available at special quantity discounts for bulk purchase for sales promotions, premiums, fund-raising, and educational needs. For details, write Charisma House Book Group, 600 Rinehart Road, Lake Mary, Florida 32746, or telephone (407) 333-0600.

THE BOOK OF MYSTERIES PRAYER JOURNAL by Jonathan Cahn
Published by FrontLine
Charisma Media/Charisma House Book Group
600 Rinehart Road
Lake Mary, Florida 32746
www.charismahouse.com

Cover design by Justin Evans

Visit the author's website at www.jonathancahn.com.

Library of Congress Control Number: 2016948078
International Standard Book Number: 978-1-62999-130-6
E-book ISBN: 978-1-62999-131-3

First edition

17 18 19 20 21 — 987654321
Printed in China

To Renata, my beloved and treasure, for her love, her encouragement, her patience, and her faithfulness, without which this book would not have been written.

To Eliel and Dael, the precious jewels and the surprise joy of our lives.

To my mother and father, for the gift of life, and for all their blessings given.

And to Him who is the Mystery of all mysteries, the Giver of all gifts, and the Gift behind them all.

CONTENTS

INTRODUCTION

HOW TO USE
THE BOOK OF MYSTERIES PRAYER JOURNAL

WELCOME TO THE prayer journal for *The Book of Mysteries* by Jonathan Cahn. This prayer journal was written for individuals wanting to go deeper in their understanding of the truths revealed in *The Book of Mysteries.* Everyone using this prayer journal should read *The Book of Mysteries* simultaneously because this prayer journal is constructed to present you with the same daily mission and scriptural foundation contained in each mystery in *The Book of Mysteries*, while providing room for journaling your study notes, prayers, or other insights that come to light as you read the original book.

At the bottom of each mystery is a title that identifies a full teaching from Jonathan that represents the full revealing of the mystery or related and parallel truths and revelations. These full teachings will take you deeper into the mystery or the explored information than space allows in *The Book of Mysteries*, and you might find it helpful to access the full teaching as you utilize this prayer journal. You can find information on ordering these teachings in the back of this book.

Whether you read several mysteries in one sitting or you use this prayer journal and its companion book, *The Book of Mysteries*, as a one-year daily devotional, we pray this journal will be a blessing to you as it provides a place for you to take time in God's presence to receive, meditate on, soak in, and apply what God will give you from His mysteries to bless, transform, and strengthen your walk and life in Him and take you deeper in your love and relationship with Him.

INFINITY IN A JAR

_____

_____

_____

_____

_____

_____

_____

_____

_____

_____

_____

_____

_____

The Mission: Today, open your mind, your heart, and your life to that which you don't yet know, that you might contain that which is greater than yourself.

Isaiah 55:1–9; Jeremiah 33:3; 2 Corinthians 4:7

THE I AM OF ALL I AMS

_____

_____

_____

_____

_____

_____

_____

_____

_____

_____

_____

_____

The Mission: Today, learn the secret of living each moment from His life, doing from His doing, loving from His love, and being from His being.

Exodus 3:14–15; Acts 17:28

The I Am Mysteries

THE SHANNAH

_____

_____

_____

_____

_____

_____

_____

_____

_____

_____

_____

_____

The Mission: Today, step out of your old ways, habits, and steps. Do what you've never done before but should have. Walk in the newness of the Spirit.

Isaiah 43:19; Romans 6:4; 2 Corinthians 5:17

THE RUACH

_____

_____

_____

_____

_____

_____

_____

_____

_____

_____

_____

The Mission: What part of your life is against the direction of the Spirit? Today, turn it around and start walking with the Wind at your back.

John 3:8; Acts 2:2; Galatians 5:16–17

Ruach

APPOINTING YOUR DAYS

The Mission: Prepare the days ahead. Set them apart. Commit them into God's hands and appoint them for the fulfilling of His purposes.

Psalm 90:12; Acts 19:21

The Shannah and the Manah

THE MYSTERY OF THE BRIDE

_____

_____

_____

_____

_____

_____

_____

_____

_____

_____

_____

_____

_____

_____

_____

The Mission: Put away anything that substitutes for His presence, and join all that you are, your deepest parts, to your Bridegroom.

Deuteronomy 6:5; Song of Solomon 1:1–4; Ephesians 5:28–32

THE POWER OF THE YUD

_____

_____

_____

_____

_____

_____

_____

_____

_____

_____

_____

_____

_____

The Mission: Today, take the smallest of actions, but in a new direction, the first step toward the life of victory you're called to live—the yud of a new journey.

Job 8:7; Acts 3:4–9

The First Step

THE MIDBAR

_____

_____

_____

_____

_____

_____

_____

_____

_____

_____

_____

_____

_____

The Mission: Put away the distractions, those things that keep you from hearing. And go into the wilderness, the midbar, and seek the voice of God.

Deuteronomy 8:2–16; Psalm 46:10; Jeremiah 29:12–13; Luke 3:2

THE SHAMAYIM AND THE ARETZ

_____

_____

_____

_____

_____

_____

_____

_____

_____

_____

_____

_____

_____

The Mission: What are your possessions? Today, let go. Free up your heart of its earthly possessions. And fill it up with the spiritual and heavenly.

Isaiah 55:9; Philippians 4:8–9

THE SERPENT'S BLOOD

_____

_____

_____

_____

_____

_____

_____

_____

_____

_____

_____

_____

The Mission: In the face of whatever evil, trouble, attack, or sin you're dealing with, don't give in. Don't give up. But press on in the good.

Isaiah 54:17; Matthew 24:13; John 1:5

THE FACE IN THE WATERS

_____

_____

_____

_____

_____

_____

_____

_____

_____

_____

_____

_____

The Mission: What is it that you seek from life and from others? Today, make it your goal to give to others the very thing you seek.

Proverbs 27:19; Luke 6:37–38; Galatians 6:7–10

THE COSMIC LOVE

_____

_____

_____

_____

_____

_____

_____

_____

_____

_____

_____

_____

The Mission: Today, practice the divine and cosmic love. Put yourself in the place of another—your feet in their shoes, your heart in their heart.

John 15:12–13; Romans 5:6–8; Philippians 2:5–9

God in Our Sandals

THE EAST-WEST CONTINUUM

_____

_____

_____

_____

_____

_____

_____

_____

_____

_____

_____

_____

The Mission: Today, take time to ponder and take in the love of God that removed your sins as far as the east is from the west—and live accordingly.

Leviticus 16:14; Psalm 103:10–12

The Mystery of the Kedem

KISSING GOD

_____

_____

_____

_____

_____

_____

_____

_____

_____

_____

_____

_____

_____

_____

_____

The Mission: Today, draw near to God in worship, in love, in joy, in the deepest of intimacy. Learn the secret of kissing God.

Psalm 42:7–8; Song of Solomon 1:2; John 4:24

Yishkeni: The Divine Kiss

THE NIGHT AND DAY PARADIGM

_____

_____

_____

_____

_____

_____

_____

_____

_____

_____

_____

_____

The Mission: What darkness is in your life, the darkness of fear, of sin, of problems, of gloom? Today, turn away from it and to the light of day.

Genesis 1:3–5; Psalm 30:5; Ephesians 5:8; 1 Peter 2:9;
2 Peter 1:19

The Night and the Sunrise

THE TALEH

_____

_____

_____

_____

_____

_____

_____

_____

_____

_____

_____

_____

The Mission: Today, live in the spirit of the Lamb. Let everything you do be done in love. And live to make your life a blessing to others.

Genesis 22:1–18; Isaiah 53:7; 1 Peter 1:18–19; Revelation 5:6–13

HOW TO ALTER YOUR PAST

_____

_____

_____

_____

_____

_____

_____

_____

_____

_____

_____

_____

_____

The Mission: Soak in the undyeing. Receive from heaven your changed, innocent, pure, and beloved past, a past as beautiful and as white as snow.

Isaiah 1:18; Luke 7:37–47; 2 Corinthians 5:21; 1 John 1:8–9

As Beloved Children

YESHUA

_____

_____

_____

_____

_____

_____

_____

_____

_____

_____

_____

_____

The Mission: God has become your Yeshua, the specific answer to your deepest needs. Let that get inside your heart and live accordingly.

Exodus 15:2; Psalm 118:14; Isaiah 12:2; Matthew 1:21

Yeshua: The Name

ALIYAH

_____

_____

_____

_____

_____

_____

_____

_____

_____

_____

_____

_____

The Mission: Today, choose the higher step, the higher act, the higher ground, the higher path in every decision. Start making your life an Aliyah.

Psalm 121; Mark 10:32

The Aliyah Mystery

THE FOOTSTOOL WORLD

_____

_____

_____

_____

_____

_____

_____

_____

_____

_____

_____

_____

The Mission: Today, see the world and everything in it in a new way, as the footstool world, with only footstool issues, and live accordingly.

Isaiah 66:1; Ephesians 2:6; Colossians 3:1–2

THE HEARTBEAT OF THE MIRACLE

_____

_____

_____

_____

_____

_____

_____

_____

_____

_____

_____

_____

_____

The Mission: Live this day in the miracle of your existence. Take account of every heartbeat and make your moments worthy of each one.

Psalm 139:14–17

THE ELOHIM MYSTERY

_____

_____

_____

_____

_____

_____

_____

_____

_____

_____

_____

_____

The Mission: Today, seek to know God as one who doesn't know the half of Him. Seek to know Him more, and afresh, as if for the first time.

Genesis 1:1; 1 Kings 8:26; Job 38

HE WHOSE NAME IS LIKE OIL

The Mission: Delight today in the name of your Beloved. Let it pour forth from your lips, your mind, and your heart.

Song of Solomon 1:3; John 1:41

Like Pure Oil

THE SECRET PLACE

_____

_____

_____

_____

_____

_____

_____

_____

_____

_____

_____

The Mission: Today, go into the secret place, apart from the world and even the *things* of Him, away from everything—but His presence.

Exodus 25:21–22; Song of Solomon 2:14; Matthew 6:6

KING OF THE CURSE

_____

_____

_____

_____

_____

_____

_____

_____

_____

_____

_____

_____

The Mission: Today, bring the thorns, the wounds, the shame, the sorrows of your life to the King of Thorns, and commit them to His authority.

Isaiah 53:3–5; 61:1–3; Matthew 27:29; Galatians 3:13

Lord of Eden

THE POWER OF EMUNAH

The Mission: Take a word from the Word of God today and give it your strongest amen, the total yes of your heart, soul, mind, and will.

Isaiah 7:9; Colossians 2:6–7; Hebrews 11:6

Emunah

THE IVRIM

_____

_____

_____

_____

_____

_____

_____

_____

_____

_____

_____

_____

The Mission: What barriers are hindering you and the will of God in your life? Identify them. Then, by the power of Messiah, begin crossing your Jordan. You are an Ivri. You were born again to cross over.

Joshua 3:14–17; John 3:3; 2 Corinthians 5:17

THE MASADA MYSTERY

_____

_____

_____

_____

_____

_____

_____

_____

_____

_____

_____

_____

The Mission: Bring your most hopeless situations and issues to God. Believe God for the impossible. Live and move in the power of the impossible.

Ezekiel 37:12–14; Luke 1:37

The Masada Mystery

THE DOUBLE

_____

_____

_____

_____

_____

_____

_____

_____

_____

_____

_____

_____

The Mission: Live today as one sentenced to judgment, but who has instead been set free and given a second chance of life, because of the love and sacrifice of Him.

Leviticus 16:7–10; Matthew 27:15–24

Azazel

THE DIVINE NONPOSSESSIVE

_____

_____

_____

_____

_____

_____

_____

_____

_____

_____

_____

_____

_____

The Mission: Today, learn the secret of living with "no have." Let go of your possessions, your problems, your burdens, your life—and possess God.

Psalm 16:5; 2 Corinthians 6:10; 1 Timothy 6:6–11

THE PORTAL

_____

_____

_____

_____

_____

_____

_____

_____

_____

_____

_____

_____

The Mission: Today, use the door of God to leave what you could never leave and go where you could never go. Enter through the portal.

Exodus 12:21–27; John 10:9; Hebrews 10:19–20

Heaven's Portal

THE TRIUNITY OF LOVE

_____

_____

_____

_____

_____

_____

_____

_____

_____

_____

_____

_____

The Mission: Partake of the triunity of love. As God has made you the object of His love, today, make those who don't deserve it become the object of yours.

Isaiah 48:16–17; Matthew 28:19–20; 1 John 4:16

Shalosh

THE DAY OF THE RESHEET

_____

_____

_____

_____

_____

_____

_____

_____

_____

_____

_____

_____

_____

_____

The Mission: If the Resheet has overcome, so then can you. Today, in full confidence of the power given you on the Day of the Resheet, overcome!

Leviticus 23:9–11; 1 Corinthians 15:20–23

The Day of New Beginnings

THE HOUSE OF BREAD

The Mission: Stop filling your needs and desires with that which is not bread. Fill your heart with the love, the presence, and the fullness of your true bread—Him.

Micah 5:2; John 6:32–35

THE ROADS OF ZION

_____

_____

_____

_____

_____

_____

_____

_____

_____

_____

_____

_____

The Mission: Today, take your eyes off your circumstances, and focus only on your destination. Press on to the good, the highest, and the heavenly.

Matthew 7:13–14; Philippians 3:12–14

The Roads of Zion Mystery

THE KHATAN

_____

_____

_____

_____

_____

_____

_____

_____

_____

_____

_____

_____

The Mission: Bring the most ungodly, dark, and untouched part of your life to the Khatan. Let Him touch it, and every part of your life.

Song of Solomon 5:10–6:2; Isaiah 54:5; 62:5; John 3:29

The Mystery of the Khatan

THE MYSTERY OF THE ZEROAH

The Mission: Today, take part in the power of the Zeroah. Let go to apprehend, surrender to overcome, and die to yourself that you might find life.

Deuteronomy 5:15; Isaiah 52:10; 53:1–5; 59:16

THE DOOR OF EVIL

_____

_____

_____

_____

_____

_____

_____

_____

_____

_____

_____

_____

The Mission: Today, make it your aim not just to avoid temptation, but to avoid even the door that leads to it. Focus on the door, and stay far from it.

Proverbs 5:3–8; 1 Corinthians 10:13

Hedges

THE CELESTIAL SEED

_____

_____

_____

_____

_____

_____

_____

_____

_____

_____

_____

_____

_____

The Mission: Today, take a seed from the Word of God and plant it in the soil of your heart. Let its promise be unlocked and bear its fruit in your life.

Matthew 13:3–23; 1 Peter 1:23

Secrets of the Sowers

THE MYSTERY OF THE SECRET ANGELS

_____

_____

_____

_____

_____

_____

_____

_____

_____

_____

_____

_____

The Mission: Today, start fulfilling your angelic mission. Bear the heavenly message to those on earth. Live this day as His earth angel.

Haggai 1:13; Malachi 3:1; Mark 16:15; Luke 7:24–27

THE NAZARENE MYSTERY

_____

_____

_____

_____

_____

_____

_____

_____

_____

_____

_____

_____

The Mission: Let Messiah's life come through your life. Let His love come through your love and your life become His branching— His Nazareth.

Zechariah 3:8; Isaiah 11:1–2; Matthew 2:23; John 15:1–5

Messiah the Branch

HOW TO MULTIPLY BREAD

_____

_____

_____

_____

_____

_____

_____

_____

_____

_____

_____

_____

The Mission: Stop seeking more and stop living in the realm of "not enough." Today, practice giving thanks for everything. Perform the act of multiplication.

Matthew 14:14–21; 1 Thessalonians 5:18

THE ASHAM

_____

_____

_____

_____

_____

_____

_____

_____

_____

_____

_____

_____

_____

The Mission: Take all the regrets, shame, and guilt you've ever carried in your life. Give them to Him who is your Asham, and let them go forever.

Isaiah 53:7–11; 2 Corinthians 5:21

THE MYSTERY OF THE RAINS

_____

_____

_____

_____

_____

_____

_____

_____

_____

_____

_____

_____

_____

The Mission: Seek the outpouring of His Spirit on your life to touch your dry ground and make it fruitful. Prepare and receive your latter rains.

Isaiah 44:3–4; Joel 2:23–29; Acts 2:17–18

THE SWORD OF AMALEK

_____

_____

_____

_____

_____

_____

_____

_____

_____

_____

_____

_____

The Mission: Whatever darkness, compromise, or ungodly thing still exists in your life, no matter how small, today, root it out. There is no middle ground.

Exodus 17:8–16; 1 Samuel 15:8–33; Esther 3:1; 2 Corinthians 2:14

HEAVEN'S MILK

_____

_____

_____

_____

_____

_____

_____

_____

_____

_____

_____

_____

The Mission: What are the deepest needs and longings of your heart? Join them to Him. Bring them to Him, and receive from Him their filling.

Ecclesiastes 3:11; Romans 8:22–23; Philippians 4:6–9

THE SIXTH DAY

_____

_____

_____

_____

_____

_____

_____

_____

_____

_____

_____

_____

The Mission: The life of man is given on the sixth day. Receive your life, your breath, and your new creation in the sixth day of Messiah.

Genesis 1:26–31; Mark 15:42–43; Ephesians 1:7

The Sixth Day Revelation Mystery

INTO THE DEEP

_____

_____

_____

_____

_____

_____

_____

_____

_____

_____

_____

The Mission: Launch out into the deep waters of God today. And there let down your net that it might break with His blessings.

Genesis 49:25; Luke 5:4–11; 1 Corinthians 2:10–13

Into the Deep

THE MYSTERY OF THE TAMID

_____

_____

_____

_____

_____

_____

_____

_____

_____

_____

_____

_____

_____

_____

_____

_____

The Mission: Meditate on the fact that Messiah is your Tamid—the covering for every moment of your life—always, and forever. Live accordingly.

Exodus 29:38–39; Mark 15:25–37; Revelation 7:9–17

THE TENT WORLD

_____

_____

_____

_____

_____

_____

_____

_____

_____

_____

_____

_____

The Mission: Live this day as a camper. Don't get caught up in your circumstances. Focus instead on the journeying. And travel lightly.

2 Corinthians 4:16–5:5; Hebrews 11:8–16

The Feast of Camping

HEAVEN'S DESCENT

_____

_____

_____

_____

_____

_____

_____

_____

_____

_____

_____

_____

_____

The Mission: Make it your aim today not to strive for heaven, but let heaven—its love, its blessings, and its joy—get into you."

Isaiah 45:8; 55:10–11; John 6:51

Jehovah of Nazareth

YAMIM NORAIM: THE DAYS OF AWE

_____

_____

_____

_____

_____

_____

_____

_____

_____

_____

_____

_____

The Mission: Look at the remainder of your days of life in a new way, as the Yamim Noraim. Get right with God and those in your life, for today is a Day of Awe.

Isaiah 55:6–7; Ephesians 5:16

The Awesome Days

GATSHMANIM

_____

_____

_____

_____

_____

_____

_____

_____

_____

_____

_____

The Mission: Today, let every desire and ambition that is not of God be surrendered and crushed. And in their crushing, be filled with the oil of the Holy Spirit.

Leviticus 8:10–12; Luke 22:39–44

The God Price

THE MYSTERY NATION

_____

_____

_____

_____

_____

_____

_____

_____

_____

_____

_____

_____

The Mission: Live this day seeking to follow His will and purposes and to bear witness of His existence in everything you do.

Genesis 17:1–8; Jeremiah 31:35–37; Ephesians 2:11–22

The Secret of His Immortality

THE WELLS OF YESHUA

_____

_____

_____

_____

_____

_____

_____

_____

_____

_____

_____

_____

_____

The Mission: Today, come to the wells of Yeshua, and in joy, draw forth and partake of the rivers of the living waters of the Spirit of God.

Isaiah 12:1–3; John 7:37–39

The Water Pouring

RACHAMIM

_____

_____

_____

_____

_____

_____

_____

_____

_____

_____

_____

The Mission: Open your heart today to receive the rachamim God has for you, not only for your sins, but the overflowing rivers of His compassions and love.

Psalm 136; Lamentations 3:22–23; Daniel 9:9; 2 Corinthians 1:3–4

Rachamim

THE MANTLE OF MESSIAH

_____

_____

_____

_____

_____

_____

_____

_____

_____

_____

_____

_____

_____

The Mission: Today, fully take up your mantle in Messiah. And by the power and the authority of the Spirit, step out to fulfill your high calling.

Deuteronomy 31:7–8; 34:9; 1 Kings 19:9; Acts 2:1–4

The Mantle

THE DAVAR AND THE OLAM

_____

_____

_____

_____

_____

_____

_____

_____

_____

_____

_____

_____

The Mission: Choose the Word over the world, over your circumstances, your problems, and everything else. Let the Davar rule your olam.

Psalm 33:6–9; John 1:1–4; Hebrews 11:3

The Word

THE EXODUS FACTOR

_____

_____

_____

_____

_____

_____

_____

_____

_____

_____

_____

The Mission: Where do you need to go? What promised land has God called you to enter? What must you first leave? Begin your exodus today.

Genesis 12:1–3; Exodus 12:51; 2 Corinthians 5:17;
Ephesians 4:22–24

The Secrets of Change & Breakthrough

THE SECRET OF YOMA

_____

_____

_____

_____

_____

_____

_____

_____

_____

_____

_____

_____

The Mission: Even the rabbis bear witness, around AD 30 the way was opened. Use the power of Messiah today to open the doors that are closed.

Psalm 24:7–10; Matthew 27:50–51; Hebrews 6:19–20; 10:19–20

The Mystery of the Temple Doors

THE REVELATION LAND

_____

_____

_____

_____

_____

_____

_____

_____

_____

_____

_____

_____

_____

_____

The Mission: Take in the revelation of Moriah personally—that if you were the only person in the world, He still would have given His life for you.

Psalm 122; Matthew 27:29–50; Romans 5:8

The Moriah Miracle

THE JONAH PARADOX

_____

_____

_____

_____

_____

_____

_____

_____

_____

_____

_____

_____

The Mission: Today, let His mercy triumph over all judgment and condemnation. Let logic of judgment yield to the paradox of His love.

Jonah 3; 2 Peter 3:9

The Book of Jonah I–VII

IN HIS DEATHS

_____

_____

_____

_____

_____

_____

_____

_____

_____

_____

_____

The Mission: One of the deaths *in His deaths* is the death of your old life. Give that which is old a eulogy and a burial. Be finished with it and be free.

Isaiah 53:9; Romans 5:18; 2 Corinthians 5:14–15

THE TALMIDIM

The Mission: Start living today as a true disciple, a learner. Seek the Rabbi's teaching. Listen to His voice and follow His instruction.

Matthew 4:18–22; Matthew 9:9; John 1:36–40

The Cosmic Rabbi

THE BIRTH TOMB

_____

_____

_____

_____

_____

_____

_____

_____

_____

_____

_____

_____

The Mission: What is it in your life that must end? Bring it into Messiah's tomb. And wait there. For after you've come to the end, you'll find the beginning.

Matthew 28:1–6; 1 Corinthians 15:55–57; 1 Peter 1:23

Yom Rishon: The Beginning of Days

THE MYSTERY PRIEST

_____

_____

_____

_____

_____

_____

_____

_____

_____

_____

_____

The Mission: The cohanim have spoken. The Lamb has been slain. And every one of your sins has been taken away. Rejoice in it. Live accordingly.

Luke 1:5–25, 57–80; 3:1–4; John 1:29

THE HAFTORAH MYSTERY

_____

_____

_____

_____

_____

_____

_____

_____

_____

_____

_____

_____

The Mission: Take a Word from Scripture you can walk in this day. Seek for the exact and appointed moments for the Word to come to fruition.

Psalm 18:30; Amos 9:11–15; 2 Timothy 3:16

The Haftorah Mystery

THE SUNSET

_____

_____

_____

_____

_____

_____

_____

_____

_____

_____

_____

_____

The Mission: Let the sun set on all in your life that is old. Let all that has been…become yesterday, forever, in the sunset of Messiah.

John 8:12; 9:5; 19:30–41

THE HOUSE OF SPIRITS

_____

_____

_____

_____

_____

_____

_____

_____

_____

_____

_____

The Mission: Move all the more away from the darkness you left. And pray all the more for the civilization in which you dwell.

Matthew 12:43–45; Luke 8:26–36; Philippians 2:15;
1 Peter 2:11–12

THE BOOK OF THE UNMENTIONED GOD

_____

_____

_____

_____

_____

_____

_____

_____

_____

_____

_____

_____

The Mission: Whenever you can't see or feel the presence of God in your life, know that He's fully there. It's just your Book of the Unmentioned God.

Psalm 139:7–12; Matthew 28:18–20; Hebrews 13:5

THE OMEGA JOY

_____

_____

_____

_____

_____

_____

_____

_____

_____

_____

_____

The Mission: Today, look to the joy at the end of your path. And so live all the more confidently in what is good and right—to the Omega joy.

Leviticus 23:33–44; Psalm 16:11; Isaiah 51:11

The Last Joy

THE OTHER TREE

_____

_____

_____

_____

_____

_____

_____

_____

_____

_____

_____

The Mission: The second tree must be the center. Make it the center of your life and center everything else around it. Partake and live of its fruit.

Genesis 2:16–17; Galatians 3:13

The Tree

THE TWO WATERS

_____

_____

_____

_____

_____

_____

_____

_____

_____

_____

_____

_____

The Mission: Live this day after the pattern of the Sea of Galilee, always receiving and always giving. Live to be a blessing in the flowing of His love.

Proverbs 11:24; Matthew 10:8; Luke 6:38; 2 Corinthians 9:6–11

The Waters of Zion

THE POEM OF GOD

_____

_____

_____

_____

_____

_____

_____

_____

_____

_____

_____

_____

The Mission: Let your life this day be led and written by God. Move at the impulse of the Author and in His flow. Live as the Poem of God.

Isaiah 43:1; Jeremiah 29:11; Ephesians 2:10

EEM-ANU-EL

The Mission: Today, practice the Hebrew of His name. In every circumstance speak and fathom the reality of eem anu El—God is with you, always.

Isaiah 7:14; Matthew 1:21–25; Luke 8:22–25

Immanuel I-II

BEYOND THE SPEED OF LIGHT

_____

_____

_____

_____

_____

_____

_____

_____

_____

_____

_____

_____

_____

The Mission: Live today not by what you see, but beyond your seeing, beyond your hearing, and beyond your sensing. Live by the unseen—by faith.

Habakkuk 2:2–4; 2 Corinthians 4:18; 5:7

THE PRIESTS OF THE OFFERING

_____

_____

_____

_____

_____

_____

_____

_____

_____

_____

_____

_____

_____

The Mission: What or who in this world is against you or working for evil? Commit it to God. And give thanks beforehand that He will turn it for good.

Leviticus 16; Matthew 20:18; Romans 8:28

SHEPHERDLESSNESS

_____

_____

_____

_____

_____

_____

_____

_____

_____

_____

_____

_____

_____

The Mission: Cease from all straying. Draw near to your Shepherd. Be fed from His hands. Rest in the protection and the tender love of His arms.

Isaiah 40:11; Ezekiel 34:5–16; Zechariah 13:7; John 10:11–16

Strike the Shepherd

THE AKEDAH MYSTERY

_____

_____

_____

_____

_____

_____

_____

_____

_____

_____

_____

_____

The Mission: Today, ponder the price of love that was paid for you, and live your life likewise as a sacrifice of love to Him.

Genesis 22; John 3:16

The Moriah Miracle

THE BRIDEGROOM'S VISITATION

_____

_____

_____

_____

_____

_____

_____

_____

_____

_____

_____

_____

The Mission: Today, encounter the Bridegroom. But instead of trying to reach Him, let Him reach you, just where you are, just as you are.

Matthew 25:1–13; John 3:29; 16:28

THE CELESTIAL CURRENCY EXCHANGE

_____

_____

_____

_____

_____

_____

_____

_____

_____

_____

_____

_____

_____

_____

_____

_____

_____

The Mission: Today, start your heavenly currency exchange. Give of
your time, your energy, your wealth, and your love to the purposes
of heaven.

Proverbs 10:2; 19:17; Matthew 6:19–21

Tithes to Jerusalem

THE WAY OF THE YASHAR

The Mission: Today, make it your aim to eliminate all wavering in your life and whatever is not in line with God's will. Walk and live in a straight line.

Isaiah 40:3–5; Hebrews 12:13

Making Straight the Crook

THE IMPOSSIBILITY OF EXISTENCE

_____

_____

_____

_____

_____

_____

_____

_____

_____

_____

_____

The Mission: Today, ponder the miracle of every moment you have. Treasure each moment and make the most of it. And make Him the cause of all you do.

Genesis 1:1–2; John 1:1–3; Hebrews 11:3

The Unknowable Love

THE KNEELING GOD

_____

_____

_____

_____

_____

_____

_____

_____

_____

_____

_____

_____

_____

The Mission: Whom do you need to bless? Be a blessing to them today. As God humbled Himself to bless you, humble yourself likewise, to become a blessing to others.

Psalm 95:6–8; Philippians 2:4–10; James 4:6–10

The Purple Crimson King I–II

THE MYSTERY OF EPHRATAH

The Mission: What gifts, resources, and abilities do you possess? Turn each one into a gift to be given and seek today every chance to give of them.

Micah 5:2; Luke 22:14–20

Ephratah: The Mystery

NISAN

The Mission: Break out of the winter and out of every darkness, and bear the fruit your life was to bear. Live in the power of Nisan.

Song of Solomon 2:8–13; 2 Corinthians 5:17

Nisan

THE SIMILITUDE

_____

_____

_____

_____

_____

_____

_____

_____

_____

_____

_____

_____

The Mission: Whatever you know of God, He's more and beyond it. So seek today to find the more and beyond of God than you have yet known.

Ezekiel 1:26–28; Philippians 3:10

The Stranger

THE PORTABLE MOUNTAINTOP

_____

_____

_____

_____

_____

_____

_____

_____

_____

_____

_____

The Mission: Today, even in the most unlikely or lowest of circumstances, set up your portable mountaintop and dwell with God on the heights.

Exodus 25:8; John 1:14

THE MYSTERY OF THE EIGHTH DAY

_____

_____

_____

_____

_____

_____

_____

_____

_____

_____

_____

_____

The Mission: Seek today to live beyond your circumstances, beyond the world, beyond the finite, in the day beyond days, in the Eighth Day.

Leviticus 23:39; Romans 6:11; 2 Corinthians 5:1–6; Revelation 20:11

The Mystery of the Eighth Day I–III

THE LAND OF GEZARAH

_____

_____

_____

_____

_____

_____

_____

_____

_____

_____

_____

_____

The Mission: Say good-bye to your sins, to your guilt, to your past, and to all that has been removed. Let it go and cut it off forever—in the land of gezarah.

Leviticus 16:21–22; Psalm 103:12; Isaiah 44:22; 53:8

Azazel

THE SHADOW

_____

_____

_____

_____

_____

_____

_____

_____

_____

_____

_____

_____

_____

The Mission: Today, practice seeing through the darkness of every problem or evil that confronts you—to the good that lies beyond it.

John 3:20–21; 8:24; 18:37

The Strategies of Warfare I–IV

THE SECRET ISRAEL

_____

_____

_____

_____

_____

_____

_____

_____

_____

_____

_____

_____

The Mission: Today, seek to find the riches of the Jewish roots of your faith and your secret identity as a spiritual Hebrew, an Israelite of God.

Genesis 12:3; John 10:16; Ephesians 2:11–22

The Israel of Spirit

THE BRIDE IN THE TENT

_____

_____

_____

_____

_____

_____

_____

_____

_____

_____

_____

_____

The Mission: Live this day as the bride in the tent—as one no longer bound by your circumstances, but belonging to the Bridegroom—free of this world.

John 17:9–18; 2 Corinthians 11:12; 1 Peter 2:11–12

The Great Preparation

THE LAW OF THE FALLOW GROUND

_____

_____

_____

_____

_____

_____

_____

_____

_____

_____

_____

_____

_____

The Mission: Identify the fallow ground in your life. Open it up to this day, to the touch of God, His Word, and His will. Let it bear its harvest.

Hosea 10:12; Matthew 13:23

Neru Lachem

THE LAMBS OF NISAN

_____

_____

_____

_____

_____

_____

_____

_____

_____

_____

_____

_____

The Mission: Bring home the Lamb to the place you really live your life, and let Him come into every room, closet, dark space, and crevice in your life.

Exodus 12:3; Matthew 21:1–11

The Nisan Lamb

THE CAPERNAUM MYSTERY

_____

_____

_____

_____

_____

_____

_____

_____

_____

_____

_____

_____

The Mission: Come to Kaphar Nachum today. Repent of anything not in His will. Then dwell in the comfort of His presence where your miracle awaits.

Isaiah 61:1–3; Matthew 4:13–16, 24

The Hands of Messiah

WHERE YOU GO

_____

_____

_____

_____

_____

_____

_____

_____

_____

_____

_____

_____

_____

The Mission: What is the direction of the calling of your life? Today, dwell only on that which leads to that destination, and on nothing that doesn't.

Proverbs 4:25–27; Philippians 3:13–14; 4:8; Ephesians 4:1

The Look Where You're Going Principle

THE FOOD OF THE PRIESTS

_____

_____

_____

_____

_____

_____

_____

_____

_____

_____

_____

The Mission: Partake today only of what is good and holy, the food of the priests. Dwell on the good and nothing else. And you will become so.

Leviticus 6:29; Psalm 34:8; John 6:51

Food of the Priests

SONG OF THE STONE

_____

_____

_____

_____

_____

_____

_____

_____

_____

_____

_____

_____

_____

_____

The Mission: Make Him who is the Cornerstone, the cornerstone of all you do today. Build everything else from that foundation.

Psalm 118:22–23; Isaiah 53:3; Hebrews 13:12–13; 1 Peter 2:4–8

The Rosh Pinah

THE MYSTERY OF THE TRIANGLES

_____

_____

_____

_____

_____

_____

_____

_____

_____

_____

_____

_____

The Mission: The blood of the Lamb breaks every chain and bondage. Walk today in the power of the Lamb and break free.

Exodus 12:3–7; 1 Corinthians 5:7

The Lamb and the Doorway

THE CHALDEAN MYSTERY

_____

_____

_____

_____

_____

_____

_____

_____

_____

_____

_____

_____

_____

The Mission: Take a promise from His Word. Believe the promise with all your heart. Step out and live your life in light of it.

Genesis 12:1–3

The Chaldean Secret of World History I–III

MIRYAM

_____

_____

_____

_____

_____

_____

_____

_____

_____

_____

_____

_____

_____

The Mission: Take up the mystery of Miryam. Make it your aim this day, to bear His life, His presence, and His joy into the world.

Exodus 2:1–9; Luke 1:26–38

Miryam

YOM RISHON: THE COSMIC BEGINNING

_____

_____

_____

_____

_____

_____

_____

_____

_____

_____

_____

_____

The Mission: Live today as if it was Day One, as if everything that should never have been, never was, and all is new. For in redemption, it is so.

Genesis 1:1; Mark 16:2–6

Yom Rishon

THE SHADOW MAN

_____

_____

_____

_____

_____

_____

_____

_____

_____

_____

_____

_____

The Mission: Joseph means he shall increase, a shadow of Messiah who, like Joseph, triumphs through all things. In Messiah, you have that same power. Use it this day.

Genesis 50:19–21; Isaiah 53; John 1:9–13

The Shadow Man I–VI

THE MAN BORN TO PAUSE AND ASK

_____

_____

_____

_____

_____

_____

_____

_____

_____

_____

_____

_____

The Mission: Today, pause, stop what you're doing, cease from your routine and your course, and with no preconceptions, seek Him.

Jeremiah 29:11–13; Acts 9:1–8; Romans 1:1

The Name of Paul

THE AUDIBLE SAPPHIRE

_____

_____

_____

_____

_____

_____

_____

_____

_____

_____

_____

The Mission: Today, make every word that comes out of your mouth a precious jewel, a gift of life, the spoken sapphire.

Ephesians 4:29; 5:19; Colossians 4:6; 1 Peter 4:11

Not a Rotten Word

THE OTHER ELOHIM

_____

_____

_____

_____

_____

_____

_____

_____

_____

_____

_____

_____

_____

The Mission: Get rid of the elohim in your life, the idols you seek after, the gods that drive you. Get rid of your elohim and return to your Elohim.

Exodus 32:7–8; Romans 1:23; 1 Thessalonians 1:9–10; 1 John 5:21

The Golden Calf Revelation I–IV

THE MAGIAN JOURNEY

_____

_____

_____

_____

_____

_____

_____

_____

_____

_____

_____

_____

_____

_____

The Mission: Today, set out on a Magian journey. Journey away from the familiar to the new as you seek more of Him, His will, and His presence.

Isaiah 60:1–6; Matthew 2:1–11

The Journey of the Magi

THE MAGNITUDE OF THE SUN

_____

_____

_____

_____

_____

_____

_____

_____

_____

_____

_____

_____

The Mission: Today, see all things in view of the big picture. Whatever problems or issues you have are small in comparison to Him and will pass away in the magnitude of the Son.

John 8:12; Ephesians 3:16–19; Hebrews 13:8

Two Thousand Years Ago

THE TWO THREE THOUSANDS

_____

_____

_____

_____

_____

_____

_____

_____

_____

_____

_____

_____

The Mission: Instead of struggling to accomplish the will of God, live, move, and be moved by the Spirit of God—and you will fulfill His will.

Exodus 32:20; Leviticus 23:15–21; Acts 2:41; 2 Corinthians 3:4–6

Tablets of the Spirit

CHAYIM

_____

_____

_____

_____

_____

_____

_____

_____

_____

_____

_____

The Mission: Remove from your life today any action or thought that which leads to death, starting with sin. Replace them with that which leads to life.

Isaiah 25:5–9; John 11:25; Acts 3:15

The Hebrew Mysteries I–IV

THE MYSTERY OF THE CHERUBIM

_____

_____

_____

_____

_____

_____

_____

_____

_____

_____

_____

The Mission: In Messiah all barriers are gone. Move forward this day in that power, through every veil, wall, separation, hindrance, and cherubim.

Genesis 3:24; Exodus 26:31; Mark 15:38; Romans 8:31–37

The Day of the Cherubim

THE MIND BINDERS

_____

_____

_____

_____

_____

_____

_____

_____

_____

_____

_____

_____

_____

The Mission: Take a word from Scripture. Dwell on it, agree with it, and bind it to your thoughts, your emotions, your heart, and your mind.

Deuteronomy 11:18; 2 Corinthians 10:4–5; 1 Peter 1:13

THE FOURTH CREATURE

_____

_____

_____

_____

_____

_____

_____

_____

_____

_____

_____

_____

The Mission: Separate your heart, your mind, your actions, and your way of life from any defilement of the present culture and anything that goes against the Word and ways of God.

Leviticus 20:26; Daniel 7:1–7; 1 Peter 2:9–12

The Iron Creature

THE SCROLL OF DAYS

_____

_____

_____

_____

_____

_____

_____

_____

_____

_____

_____

_____

_____

The Mission: Make the Word of God the plan for your day. Focus on fulfilling His Word over anything else, and you will be led to His perfect will.

Psalm 139:16; Jeremiah 29:11; Ephesians 2:10

THE OHEL MOED

_____

_____

_____

_____

_____

_____

_____

_____

_____

_____

_____

_____

The Mission: Today, build and place your tent of meeting in the center of your day and life, and place the rest of your day and life around it.

Exodus 25:8–9; Matthew 6:6, 33

The Mishkan Kit I–II

THE HUPOGRAMMOS

_____

_____

_____

_____

_____

_____

_____

_____

_____

_____

_____

_____

The Mission: Don't just go through this day, but seek first the hupogrammos of your day. Receive your actions and steps from Him—and then trace them.

Ephesians 5:1–2; 1 Peter 2:21

The Hupogrammos

THE COSMIC BRIDAL CHAMBER

_____

_____

_____

_____

_____

_____

_____

_____

_____

_____

_____

_____

_____

The Mission: Live today as one preparing for the wedding. Use every moment as a chance to become more beautiful and heavenly.

Isaiah 52:1–2; Ephesians 5:26–27; Revelation 21:2

THE COVENANT OF THE BROKEN

_____

_____

_____

_____

_____

_____

_____

_____

_____

_____

_____

_____

The Mission: As much as you've failed, get up. As much as you've fallen, get up. He redeems that which is broken. Go and do likewise.

Jeremiah 31:31–34; Hosea 14:4–7; John 8:9–11

The Brit Haddashah

THE MYSTERY OF THE SEMIKHAH

_____

_____

_____

_____

_____

_____

_____

_____

_____

_____

_____

_____

_____

The Mission: The Semikhah has been performed. Therefore, live this day as one whose sins have been absolutely, for certain, and for real, taken away forever.

Leviticus 16:21; Mark 14:65

Footsteps on the Altar

THE SHERESH

_____

_____

_____

_____

_____

_____

_____

_____

_____

_____

_____

_____

The Mission: Focus today on strengthening your roots, going deeper in God's presence, deeper in receiving. And from those roots, bear your fruit.

Psalm 1:3; Proverbs 12:12; Colossians 2:6–7

Radically Rooted

THE ANTI-WITNESS

_____

_____

_____

_____

_____

_____

_____

_____

_____

_____

_____

_____

The Mission: Today, believe, take courage, and live confidently in the truth that the good will, in the end, prevail over all evil—in the world and in your life.

Ezekiel 34:5–8; 1 Peter 5:8–9; Revelation 12:9–17

The Dragon's Secret and the Plans of Heaven I–II

THE MYSTERY OF SPRING

The Mission: Live this day in the springtime of salvation. Leave the old. Come back to the new. For in the Passover Lamb it is always springtime.

Song of Solomon 2:10–13; Romans 6:4; Revelation 21:5

Nisan

THE SEVENTH DAY

_____

_____

_____

_____

_____

_____

_____

_____

_____

_____

_____

_____

The Mission: Leave the sixth day. Leave your struggling, your laboring, and your works. And come to the Sabbath of Messiah. Enter the seventh day.

Genesis 2:2–3; Matthew 11:28; Hebrews 4:4–11

Adon Ha Shabbat

THE TEMPLE LAMBS

_____

_____

_____

_____

_____

_____

_____

_____

_____

_____

_____

_____

The Mission: Messiah's entire life was a living sacrifice, every moment a gift given, the incarnation of love. Be and do likewise.

Micah 5:2; Luke 2:8–20

THE MYSTERY HARVESTS

_____

_____

_____

_____

_____

_____

_____

_____

_____

_____

_____

_____

The Mission: Live today in the way of the kingdom. Before you see the blessing, rejoice and give thanks for it. Celebrate your mystery harvest.

Deuteronomy 16:15; Jeremiah 31:3–6; Mark 11:24

THE DAYS OF FUTURE PAST

_____

_____

_____

_____

_____

_____

_____

_____

_____

_____

The Mission: Live this day in the Hebrew perfect. Do all things from His finished work. Triumph from the victory already won. Live from the completion.

Matthew 5:48; Ephesians 2:10; Philippians 3:13–15

The Hebrew Mysteries I–IV

DUNAMAHEE: THE POWER OF I CAN

_____

_____

_____

_____

_____

_____

_____

_____

_____

_____

_____

_____

The Mission: Live this day in the dunamahee of God. Whatever you have to do in the will of God, claim the power of I can. And in that power, *do it.*

Zechariah 4:6–9; Luke 24:49; Philippians 4:13

THE PROMISE

_____

_____

_____

_____

_____

_____

_____

_____

_____

_____

_____

_____

_____

_____

The Mission: Today, find a promise in the Word of God that applies to you and stand on it, believe it, and live this day in light of it.

Jeremiah 30–31; 2 Corinthians 1:20

KINGDOM OF THE LAMB

_____

_____

_____

_____

_____

_____

_____

_____

_____

_____

_____

The Mission: Live this day in the way of the Lamb. Let go that you might have. Die that you might live. And surrender that you might overcome.

Matthew 5:30–45; 20:25–28; 2 Corinthians 6:3–10; 12:9–10;
Revelation 5:6–14

The Lamb Mysteries I–VI

THE UNSCRIPTURES

_____

_____

_____

_____

_____

_____

_____

_____

_____

_____

_____

_____

The Mission: Today, join the Word to the parchment of your heart, your will, your emotions, and your ways. Let your life become the sacred white of God's Word.

Psalm 119:11; Matthew 7:24; Colossians 3:16

THE BISORAH

_____

_____

_____

_____

_____

_____

_____

_____

_____

_____

_____

_____

The Mission: Receive today the Bisorah, the good news, as if for the first time. And by that power walk afresh in the newness of life.

Proverbs 25:25; Isaiah 52:7; 61:1

The Nisan Gospel Mystery

THE PRIVATE AND THE GENERAL

The Mission: Today, aim to walk fully in the will of God. Carry out a mission from the General. And as you walk in His will, walk also in His authority.

Matthew 28:18–20; John 20:21–23; 2 Corinthians 10:3–5

THE SKELETON PROPHECY

_____

_____

_____

_____

_____

_____

_____

_____

_____

_____

_____

_____

The Mission: Even modern history bears it witness: God is the God of the impossible. Seeing the reality, believe God today for the impossible.

Ezekiel 37:1–14; Luke 1:37

The Valley of Dry Bones Revelation

THE PREEMPTOR

The Mission: Today, respond to any problem, setback, hindrance, or attack by pressing on all the more to apprehend the victory that lies just beyond it.

2 Corinthians 2:11, 14; Hebrews 10:36

THE HEAVEN-TO-EARTH LIFE

_____

_____

_____

_____

_____

_____

_____

_____

_____

_____

_____

_____

The Mission: Learn the secret today of living a heaven-to-earth life. Live each moment *from* above, *from* the good, *from* the glorious, *from* heaven.

Isaiah 55:10–11; Matthew 6:10; Colossians 3:2

As It Is in Heaven

SHALOM ALEICHEM

_____

_____

_____

_____

_____

_____

_____

_____

_____

_____

_____

_____

The Mission: Today, make it your aim to receive the shalom of Messiah—His peace, fullness, rest, completion, well-being, and wholeness. Shalom Aleichem.

Isaiah 53:5; John 20:19–21; Colossians 3:15

The Shalom I Give

THE LEPER KING

_____

_____

_____

_____

_____

_____

_____

_____

_____

_____

_____

_____

The Mission: Even the rabbis bear witness: Messiah has taken your sins, your infirmities, your sorrows, and your condemnation. Today, let Him have them.

Isaiah 53:4–8; Matthew 8:16–17; 1 Peter 2:22–24

THE APOKALUPSIS

_____

_____

_____

_____

_____

_____

_____

_____

_____

_____

_____

_____

The Mission: Come to God today in the apokalupsis of the bride, unveiled, nothing hidden, and nothing covered. Let Him touch what must be touched.

1 Corinthians 13:12; Ephesians 5:27; Revelation 13:1; 19:7–9

The Person Behind the Veil

THE SECRET OF COLORS

_____

_____

_____

_____

_____

_____

_____

_____

_____

_____

_____

The Mission: Commit to become a vessel of giving, to fully give of every blessing. Start today. And your life will become the reflection of God.

Proverbs 11:25–26; Matthew 5:16; 2 Corinthians 3:18

THE POWER OF THE AXE

_____

_____

_____

_____

_____

_____

_____

_____

_____

_____

_____

_____

The Mission: Today, sharpen your axe. Focus your life. Make God and His purposes the point, the aim, and the goal of everything you do.

Ecclesiastes 10:10; 1 Corinthians 9:24–27; Colossians 3:17

Sharp

RECHEM AND RACHAM

_____

_____

_____

_____

_____

_____

_____

_____

_____

_____

_____

_____

The Mission: Take time today to dwell in the racham, the deep compassions and tender mercies of the Lord. Let it change you into His image.

Isaiah 44:24; John 3:3–8

Rachamim

TZEMACH: THE BRANCH MAN

_____

_____

_____

_____

_____

_____

_____

_____

_____

_____

_____

_____

The Mission: Is He greater in your life than before? Today, make Him greater in your heart, your mind, your ways, and your love.

Zechariah 6:12; Philippians 2:9

The Tzemach

THE SUNRISE COMMANDMENT

_____

_____

_____

_____

_____

_____

_____

_____

_____

_____

_____

_____

The Mission: Live like the sun today, as the light. Shine God's love on all, regardless of people and circumstances. Shine rather because you're the light.

Isaiah 60:1–3; Matthew 5:14–16, 44–45

THE SILENCE OF THE TRUTH

_____

_____

_____

_____

_____

_____

_____

_____

_____

_____

_____

_____

The Mission: Today, leave the "realm of the about" and go beyond the talk and words to the bare truth of His presence. Be still and know that He is God.

Psalm 46:10; John 18:38

Him

THE WINGS OF MESSIAH

_____

_____

_____

_____

_____

_____

_____

_____

_____

_____

_____

_____

The Mission: Touch God today with the darkest, most painful, most ungodly part of your life—that you might find healing in His wings.

Numbers 15:38–40; Malachi 4:2; Matthew 9:20–22; 14:35–36

THE MYSTERY OF THE YEHUDIM

_____

_____

_____

_____

_____

_____

_____

_____

_____

_____

_____

_____

_____

The Mission: Today, praise God, give thanks, and bless. No matter what the circumstance, no matter what goes on around you or against you, praise God.

Psalm 34:1–3; Romans 2:29; Philippians 4:11–13

The Yehudim

THE AVANIM: WEIGHTS OF THE BALANCE

_____

_____

_____

_____

_____

_____

_____

_____

_____

_____

_____

_____

The Mission: Conform today your will to the truth, your ways to the Word, and your life to the image of God. Uphold the weights of the balance.

Proverbs 11:1; 16:11; Isaiah 5:20

The Weights of the Bag

THE SUMMER FRUITS

_____

_____

_____

_____

_____

_____

_____

_____

_____

_____

_____

_____

_____

The Mission: The apostles were the firstfruits. Live this day in their anointing and power, to spread the light, to touch the earth, and overcome the world.

Leviticus 23:16–17; Acts 2:2–4, 39; Galatians 5:16, 22–25

The Passover-Shavuot Resurrection Power

MOVING THE UNIVERSE

_____

_____

_____

_____

_____

_____

_____

_____

_____

_____

_____

_____

The Mission: Think of your answered prayers. God worked everything together to make it happen. Ponder that love, that He would move the world to bless you.

Genesis 24:1–28; Romans 8:28, 32

The Isaac Rebekah Wedding Mystery I–III

THE MYSTERY WRESTLER

_____

_____

_____

_____

_____

_____

_____

_____

_____

_____

_____

_____

The Mission: Is there something you're wrestling with God about, or resisting? Surrender today to His will. And in that surrender, ask for His blessing.

Genesis 32:24–30; Ephesians 2:12, 19

Messiah in the Torah

SECRET OF THE LILIES

_____

_____

_____

_____

_____

_____

_____

_____

_____

_____

_____

_____

The Mission: Today, don't focus on your works. But learn instead the secret of becoming His work. Become today the work of God.

Psalm 139:14; 149:41; Luke 12:27–31

THE PRIESTS IN THE WATERS

_____

_____

_____

_____

_____

_____

_____

_____

_____

_____

_____

_____

_____

The Mission: The priesthood has been given to Messiah and to those who are His. Live this day as a priest of God. Minister His will and purposes.

Jeremiah 31:31–33; Matthew 3:13–16

THE CHILDREN OF EVE

_____

_____

_____

_____

_____

_____

_____

_____

_____

_____

_____

_____

The Mission: Remember how God used emptiness, pain, and brokenness to bring you to life. So let every pain of this life become the pangs of birth.

Genesis 3:16; Romans 8:22–23

The Children of Eden Mysteries I–IV

THE HOUSE OF THE BRIDEGROOM

The Mission: Dwell on the blessings of the place being prepared for you. Meditate on the house of the Bridegroom. Dwell in the heavenlies.

John 14:2–3; 1 Corinthians 2:9

The Great Preparation

BARUCH ATAH

_____

_____

_____

_____

_____

_____

_____

_____

_____

_____

_____

_____

The Mission: Set your heart today on two words: *baruch* and *atah*. Purpose to be a blessing. Live not for the self but for the Atah, the "You."

Psalm 103; Matthew 22:36–40

THE DOER

_____

_____

_____

_____

_____

_____

_____

_____

_____

_____

_____

_____

The Mission: Let God become the doer of your works, and you become the doer of His works. Whatever you do, let Him do it in you.

Genesis 39:22; Isaiah 53:12; Philippians 2:13–14; 4:13

The Shadow Man I–VI

THE AFIKOMEN MYSTERY

_____

_____

_____

_____

_____

_____

_____

_____

_____

_____

_____

_____

The Mission: What in your life is still incomplete? Instead of trying to fill it, find your completion in Him, and let His fullness fill what is empty.

Zechariah 12:10; Luke 22:19; Romans 11:25–26

The Bread and the Wine

YERUSHALAYIM

_____

_____

_____

_____

_____

_____

_____

_____

_____

_____

_____

_____

The Mission: You are a child of Yerushalayim. Therefore, choose to live this day not as you are, but as you will yet be, the perfect and the heavenly.

Psalms 122; 147:2–3; Revelation 21:1–2

Yerushalayim: The Mystery

THE COSMIC CONFESSION

_____

_____

_____

_____

_____

_____

_____

_____

_____

_____

_____

_____

_____

The Mission: He became sin—your sin, that you would become righteousness—His righteousness. Live today as the righteousness of God.

Genesis 3:5; Leviticus 16:21; Mark 14:63–64; 2 Corinthians 5:21

THE MYSTERY OF THE SECOND SCROLL

The Mission: Be a Ruth today. Pray for and bless your Naomi. Pray and bless Israel and the Jewish people. Help bring their story to completion.

Ruth 1:16–17; 4:13–17; Isaiah 40:1–2; Romans 11:11; 15:26–27

The Bethlehem Allegory

THE GIFT OF THE LAHMED

_____

_____

_____

_____

_____

_____

_____

_____

_____

_____

_____

_____

The Mission: Give up 'having.' Take no good thing today for granted, every blessing, even our life. And receive everything as a gift from God.

2 Corinthians 6:10; Ephesians 5:20; James 1:17

The Divine Nonpossessive

THE APPOINTED

_____

_____

_____

_____

_____

_____

_____

_____

_____

_____

_____

_____

_____

_____

The Mission: Today, see your problems and challenges in a new way, as God's appointed ministers to bring you to the place of His will and destiny.

1 Chronicles 9:28; Jonah 1:17; 4:6–8; Psalm 139:16;
2 Thessalonians 1:11

The Book of Jonah I–VII

THE ZICHARYAH MAN

_____

_____

_____

_____

_____

_____

_____

_____

_____

_____

_____

The Mission: Remember the times when you've fallen—and yet when God didn't give up on you. In view of that dedicate your life to blessing Him all the more.

Psalm 98:3; Isaiah 49:14–16; Zechariah 8:3–9

Zechariah: God Remembers

THE LULAV

_____

_____

_____

_____

_____

_____

_____

_____

_____

_____

_____

_____

_____

The Mission: Today, gather your lulav. Remember and give thanks that in all your valleys, mountains, and deserts He was there—and always will be.

Psalm 23; Isaiah 43:1–2; Jude 1:24–25

THE SECRET OF THE BLESSED LIFE

_____

_____

_____

_____

_____

_____

_____

_____

_____

_____

_____

_____

_____

The Mission: The blessings of God are pouring down. Open your heart and life to receive them. Focus on receiving that which is already given.

Genesis 27:15–29; Ephesians 1:3–12, 18–20

The Blessing

THE TEMPLES OF DESECRATION

_____

_____

_____

_____

_____

_____

_____

_____

_____

_____

_____

_____

The Mission: Today, celebrate your own Chanukah. Remove the idols. Cleanse your chambers. Rededicate and reconsecrate your temple to God.

Ezekiel 36:25–27; John 10:22–23; 1 Corinthians 3:16; 2 Corinthians 6:16–7:1

Rededicating the Temple

THE LAW OF COSMIC MOTION

_____

_____

_____

_____

_____

_____

_____

_____

_____

_____

_____

_____

The Mission: Today, seek to receive the cosmic motion of God's love, God's life, and God's salvation. And let it change the motion and course of your life.

Ephesians 2:1–9; 1 Peter 2:9–10; 1 John 3:16

Apprehending the Momentum of Heaven I–II

THE MOON BRIDE

_____

_____

_____

_____

_____

_____

_____

_____

_____

_____

_____

_____

The Mission: Today, turn your focus away from yourself and to Him. Let your imperfections be lost in His radiance. And let your life shine with the light of His beauty.

Exodus 34:29; Song of Solomon 6:10; John 3:2; 2 Corinthians 3:18

She Like the Moon

THE SERPENT AND THE HEDGE

_____

_____

_____

_____

_____

_____

_____

_____

_____

_____

_____

_____

The Mission: What is it that is precious in your life and that you need to protect? Build strong hedges around it and, having done so, don't break the hedge.

Proverbs 22:5; Ecclesiastes 10:8; 1 Peter 2:11; 5:8–9

Snake Busters I–VI

THE SEPARATION OF THE PRIEST

The Mission: Today, give thanks for all those things that brought you to God—even the heartaches—as the holy separation of the priest.

Exodus 28:1–2; Ezekiel 44:16; 2 Timothy 1:9; 1 Peter 2:9

The Priest's Separation

THE PROPHECY NAME

_____

_____

_____

_____

_____

_____

_____

_____

_____

_____

_____

_____

The Mission: What is your prophecy name? Live by it today. Start with what the Word declares you to be: Beloved, Royal, Holy, and Victorious.

Genesis 1:3; 17:5; Matthew 6:18; Revelation 2:17

THE PERUSHIM

_____

_____

_____

_____

_____

_____

_____

_____

_____

_____

_____

The Mission: Come to Him this day as a little child, as knowing nothing, and having all to know, as having nothing, and having everything to receive.

Isaiah 57:15; Mathew 16:6; 23:2–3; Luke 7:37–48

Fasting for Nothing

THE GOSPEL-ACTS CONTINUUM

_____

_____

_____

_____

_____

_____

_____

_____

_____

_____

_____

_____

_____

The Mission: Today, let the Gospel produce the acts of God in your life. And let all your acts proceed from the good news. Get wholly into the Gospel and you will enter the Book of Acts.

Isaiah 61:1; John 21:25–Acts 2; James 2:17–26

The Sequel

THE MYSTERY OF SUMMER

_____

_____

_____

_____

_____

_____

_____

_____

_____

_____

_____

_____

The Mission: It is the summer of the age. Make it your aim this day to reap the harvest all around you. Bring forth salvation and bring in eternal life.

Proverbs 10:5; John 4:35–36; Matthew 9:37–38

The Joy of the Harvest

HA MAKOM: THE PLACE

_____

_____

_____

_____

_____

_____

_____

_____

_____

_____

_____

_____

The Mission: Bring every unanswered question, every unmet need, and every unfulfilled longing to Calvary, Mount Moriah, the place of God's providing.

Genesis 22:7–8, 14; Luke 23:33; John 1:29

The Moriah Miracle

THE ALPHA OMEGA MAN

_____

_____

_____

_____

_____

_____

_____

_____

_____

_____

_____

_____

The Mission: This day make Him your Alpha. Receive every moment from Him. And live every moment to Him as your Omega.

Isaiah 44:6; Revelation 22:13

The Alpha Stone

THE ALTAR OUTSIDE THE HOLY PLACE

_____

_____

_____

_____

_____

_____

_____

_____

_____

_____

_____

_____

_____

The Mission: You dwell in heaven's outer court, the place of sacrifice. Therefore, the life you live here must be one of sacrifice, a life of love. Begin today.

2 Chronicles 7:7; Romans 12:1; Hebrews 13:10–13

THE BAALIM

_____

_____

_____

_____

_____

_____

_____

_____

_____

_____

_____

The Mission: Identify your Baal, that which has mastered you. Submit to the will of the Master and you'll have the power to break free from that Baal.

Judges 2:11–13; 1 Kings 18:20–39; Hosea 2:16–23; 1 John 5:21

The Mask of the Gods

THE MYSTERY BREAD

_____

_____

_____

_____

_____

_____

_____

_____

_____

_____

_____

_____

The Mission: Today, partake of the bread of heaven. Seek the mahnah of His Word, the mahnah of His love, and the "What is it?" of your salvation.

Exodus 16:14–18, 30–31; John 6:32–35

Mannah

THE MAZMERAH

The Mission: What losses have you known in your life? God has used and will use them to bring good and new life. Do likewise. Use them for good.

Psalm 92:13–14; John 15:1–5

The Secrets of Pruning I–III

THE MYSTERY OF THE KEHILAH

_____

_____

_____

_____

_____

_____

_____

_____

_____

_____

_____

_____

The Mission: Live today as on a spiritual caravan. Your goal is to move continually forward, away from Egypt and closer to the Promised Land.

Exodus 16:10; Acts 7:38; 1 Peter 2:9–10

The Two Kehilahs

THE CHIASMA

_____

_____

_____

_____

_____

_____

_____

_____

_____

_____

_____

_____

_____

The Mission: Live today as if you were one of the believer at the very beginning. As they overcame their world, overcome yours.

Matthew 20:16; 23:12; 24:12–13; Acts 2:17

THE IDUMEAN MYSTERY

_____

_____

_____

_____

_____

_____

_____

_____

_____

_____

_____

The Mission: Have you lived trying to compensate for the lack of a blessing? Stop striving. Focus today on fully receiving your blessing from God.

Genesis 27:27–14; Matthew 2:1–18; Ephesians 5:1

THE IMAGE OF THEIR KING

_____

_____

_____

_____

_____

_____

_____

_____

_____

_____

_____

_____

_____

The Mission: Today, make it your first priority and aim to be conformed to the image of your King. Walk, act, think, and become in the likeness of Messiah.

Isaiah 53:3; Romans 8:29; 1 Peter 2:21

The Isaiah 53 Rabbinical Mystery I–II

THE AGENT

_____

_____

_____

_____

_____

_____

_____

_____

_____

_____

_____

_____

The Mission: Live today in the awareness that you are not alone. God Himself dwells with you in the Spirit. Live as one with whom He is present.

Genesis 24:2–4; John 14:14, 26; 15:26; 16:13

The Isaac Rebekah Wedding Mystery I–III

THE NIGHT OF ADAM

_____

_____

_____

_____

_____

_____

_____

_____

_____

_____

_____

_____

_____

The Mission: Messiah took upon Himself the curse of man. By the power of His redemption, live now against and beyond all curses, and in the blessing.

Genesis 3:19; Luke 22:19, 39–46; 1 Corinthians 15:21–22

Lord of Eden

THE POWER TO CAST A FOREST

_____

_____

_____

_____

_____

_____

_____

_____

_____

_____

_____

_____

The Mission: Today, practice dealing with every sin and temptation in its seed form and moment. Throw it out, and be glad. You just cast a forest!

Deuteronomy 29:18; Hebrews 12:14–15; James 1:14–15

The Sledgehammer Principle

THE COSMIC DICE

_____

_____

_____

_____

_____

_____

_____

_____

_____

_____

_____

_____

The Mission: Ponder those events of your life over which you've never had peace. Be at peace and give thanks that He will work all these things for your good.

Esther 9:26–28; Romans 8:28

The Purim

NIGLATAH: THE BARING

_____

_____

_____

_____

_____

_____

_____

_____

_____

_____

_____

_____

The Mission: Today, fight your battles, overcome, and win your victories—not by your strength, but by God's naked arm, the power of His love.

Isaiah 53:1; John 19:23–24; 1 John 3:16

SEEING THE COLORS OF HEAVEN

_____

_____

_____

_____

_____

_____

_____

_____

_____

_____

_____

_____

The Mission: Take judgment and hell for granted and the fact that you're saved from it, and every other blessing in your life as total undeserved grace. And, by this, live a heavenly life.

Romans 5:8; 1 Timothy 1:15–17; James 1:17; 1 John 3:1

The Third Practice

THE SECRET OF THE MAKHZOR

_____

_____

_____

_____

_____

_____

_____

_____

_____

_____

_____

_____

_____

_____

The Mission: God is present even when you don't realize it or sense that He is. Take time today to dwell in stillness that you might know and behold the presence of the Lord.

Isaiah 53:4–5; Romans 5:11; 1 Corinthians 3:11

The Rabbinic Mysteries I–VI *

THE IMMANUEL SOLUTION

_____

_____

_____

_____

_____

_____

_____

_____

_____

_____

_____

_____

The Mission: Apply this day the Immanuel Solution. Overcome the problem with the Answer, the bitterness with forgiveness, hate with love, and evil with the good.

Isaiah 7:14; Luke 6:26–36; Romans 12:9–21

THE SHEVAT: THE CEASING OF GOD

_____

_____

_____

_____

_____

_____

_____

_____

_____

_____

_____

_____

The Mission: Learn the secret of shevat. Cease with God from laboring, struggling, and from yourself. Enter the Shabbat, the Second Sabbath.

Genesis 2:2–3; John 19:30–31; Hebrews 4:4, 9–10

The Sabbath Entrance

KHANANYAH

_____

_____

_____

_____

_____

_____

_____

_____

_____

_____

_____

_____

_____

_____

The Mission: In all things today look to see khananyah, the grace of God. Follow it, dwell in it, act in it, and let everything flow out of it.

Psalm 84:11; Acts 9:8–18; 20:24; 1 Corinthians 15:10

The Power of Being Wrong

NEKHUSHTAN: THE DOUBLE NEGATIVE REDEMPTION

_____

_____

_____

_____

_____

_____

_____

_____

_____

_____

_____

_____

The Mission: Live today in the power of the double negative redemption. Doubt the doubt, defy the defiance, bind the bondage, reject the rejection, defeat the defeat, and turn death into life.

Numbers 21:8–9; John 3:14–15; Romans 8–3; 1 Corinthians 15:26; 2 Corinthians 5:21; Ephesians 4:8

THE ARCH OF TITUS

_____

_____

_____

_____

_____

_____

_____

_____

_____

_____

_____

_____

The Mission: Identify the "Arches of Titus" in your life—all the bad that God redeemed for your good. Take part in turning the present bad into blessing.

Genesis 50:19–20; Psalm 30:11–12; Romans 8:28

THE INFINITY SOLUTION

_____

_____

_____

_____

_____

_____

_____

_____

_____

_____

_____

_____

The Mission: Seek this day to live not limited by the limitations of your circumstances, problems, thoughts, and ways. Live by faith beyond them.

1 Kings 8:27; Isaiah 40:28; Romans 11:33

THE EUCHARISTIA

_____

_____

_____

_____

_____

_____

_____

_____

_____

_____

_____

_____

The Mission: Seek today not to increase what you have, but to increase your thanks for what you have. Give thanks in all things. The greater your thanksgiving, the greater will be your life.

Psalm 136; Luke 22:14–23; 1 Timothy 6:6–8

YOVEL

The Mission: Make today your Yovel. Walk in the power of freedom, restoration, reconciliation, and release. Live the power of Jubilee.

Leviticus 25:10–11; Luke 4:18–19; Galatians 5:1

Jubilee

THE ADERET

_____

_____

_____

_____

_____

_____

_____

_____

_____

_____

_____

_____

The Mission: Today, embrace the aderet, your mantle. Accept its greatness and that it's over and above you. Believe it, and, by God, rise to it.

1 Kings 19:19; 1 Corinthians 1:26–31; 2 Corinthians 3:5–6; Ephesians 4:1

Don the Mantle

YARDEN: THE DESCENDER

_____

_____

_____

_____

_____

_____

_____

_____

_____

_____

_____

_____

The Mission: As God descended in Messiah the Descender in order to bless us, so today descend, go lower, pour out your life that you might bless others.

Ephesians 4:8–10; Philippians 2:3–9; James 4:10

The Waters of Zion

THE DANCE OF THE CIRCLES

_____

_____

_____

_____

_____

_____

_____

_____

_____

_____

_____

_____

The Mission: Take part in the khag. Live your life today as an act of worship, a flowing of His love, a dance of joy.

Psalm 149:1–3; Jeremiah 31:13; 1 Corinthians 10:31

The Dance of the Heavenly Circles

THE CHRYSALIS

_____

_____

_____

_____

_____

_____

_____

_____

_____

_____

_____

_____

The Mission: Move away from the earthbound—everything in your life that is tied to the world, to the flesh, and sin. Move into the realm of the heavenly. Start flying.

Romans 6:4–8; 2 Corinthians 5:17; Galatians 2:20;
Ephesians 4:22–32

The Gospel of the Butterfly

ZICHARYAH, ELISHEVAH, AND YOCHANAN

_____

_____

_____

_____

_____

_____

_____

_____

_____

_____

_____

_____

_____

The Mission: The Scriptures are filled with promises for His people. Take one today. Hold to it. Live in light of it.

Leviticus 26:40–42; Luke 1:4–17, 72–73

The Angel and the Priest

THE MYSTERY OF EUROPA

_____

_____

_____

_____

_____

_____

_____

_____

_____

_____

_____

_____

The Mission: See behind the temptation to the destruction that awaits. Turn from all temptations, gods, idols, and sins. Love God with all your heart.

2 Timothy 3:1–5, 12; 4:1–5

The Woman, the Beast, and the Saints: The Maccabee Blueprint

HEAVEN'S LADDER

_____

_____

_____

_____

_____

_____

_____

_____

_____

_____

_____

_____

_____

The Mission: Wherever you are there is a ladder connecting you to the Most High. Find the first rung of heaven's ladder and take it.

Genesis 28:10–17; John 1:51

ANI LO

_____

_____

_____

_____

_____

_____

_____

_____

_____

_____

_____

_____

The Mission: Today live out the words Ani Lo. Live as one totally belonging to your Beloved. Make Him the aim and purpose of all you do. Give yourself to Him.

Song of Solomon 2:16; Romans 14:7–8; 1 Corinthians 6:19–20; Colossians 3:17

Ani Lo

THE SCARLET REDEMPTION

_____

_____

_____

_____

_____

_____

_____

_____

_____

_____

_____

_____

_____

_____

The Mission: See all the sins and errors of your life as turning from scarlet to white. Seek now to live a scarlet-free life, in the white of your cleansing.

Isaiah 1:18; Hebrews 10:10–14, 18–22

The Yoma Mysteries

GALILEE OF THE BROKEN

_____

_____

_____

_____

_____

_____

_____

_____

_____

_____

_____

_____

The Mission: What in your life is broken or not whole? Bring it to the Messiah of Galilee. Let Him see it. Let Him touch it. And let Him heal it.

Isaiah 9:1–2; Matthew 4:13–16; Mark 2:16–17

Galilee

THE NINTH OF AV MYSTERY

_____

_____

_____

_____

_____

_____

_____

_____

_____

_____

_____

_____

The Mission: Messiah wept for His people. Share of His heart and pray for the Jewish people, for their redemption and their return to their Shepherd.

Lamentations 1:1, 17; Ezekiel 11:17; Luke 19:41–44; 21:24

The Ninth of Av Mystery

THE RESISTANCE SECRET

_____

_____

_____

_____

_____

_____

_____

_____

_____

_____

The Mission: Today, embrace the resistance. Seek out that which will challenge you, stretch you, grow you, and strengthen you in the Lord.

Romans 5:3–5; James 1:2–4

THE MATRIX

_____

_____

_____

_____

_____

_____

_____

_____

_____

_____

_____

_____

_____

The Mission: Take all the unfulfilled longings, needs, and desires of your life and turn them away from the worldly and to the heavenly.

Psalm 139:13–16; Romans 8:22

The Matrix World

THE GREEK REDEMPTION

_____

_____

_____

_____

_____

_____

_____

_____

_____

_____

_____

_____

_____

The Mission: What part of your life has the darkness attacked? Take that very thing and use it to for the purposes, the salvation, and the glory of God.

Genesis 12:1–3; Matthew 1:1; Romans 8:28

The Chaldean Secret of World History I–III

GOD IN THE IMAGE OF MAN

_____

_____

_____

_____

_____

_____

_____

_____

_____

_____

_____

_____

The Mission: Messiah, in His death, took upon Himself your image. Now take upon yourself His image. Live today in the image and nature of God.

Genesis 1:26–27; Matthew 27:27–37; 2 Corinthians 5:21; Galatians 3:13

The Sixth Day Revelation Mystery

DODEKHA: THE DIVINE LOVES

_____

_____

_____

_____

_____

_____

_____

_____

_____

_____   _____

_____

_____

The Mission: Seek this day to know not only the love but the *loves* of God—the always new and never-ending loves of your Beloved for you.

Psalm 63:3–6; Song of Solomon 1:2; Ephesians 3:18–19

STARWOMAN

_____

_____

_____

_____

_____

_____

_____

_____

_____

_____

_____

_____

The Mission: Live this day as a heavenly light. Live as a living sacrifice, a gift given for the purposes of God. And you'll shine as the stars.

Esther 2:7; 4:16; Daniel 12:3; Matthew 10:39; Philippians 2:16

The Power of Perishing

THE PIDYON HA BEN

_____

_____

_____

_____

_____

_____

_____

_____

_____

_____

_____

_____

The Mission: Messiah is your Pidyon Ha Ben, the redemption and ransom for your life. Live as one ransomed, redeemed, free, and indebted to love.

Numbers 3:44–48; Matthew 26:14–16

The Pidyon Mystery

FROM THE DAYS OF FOREVER

_____

_____

_____

_____

_____

_____

_____

_____

_____

_____

_____

_____

The Mission: Ponder the love that God has for you that has already endured for an eternity, and will not cease or fail you now. Live accordingly.

Psalm 103:17; Jeremiah 31:3; Micah 5:2

The From Forever Redemption

THE DAY OF THE MATTAN

_____

_____

_____

_____

_____

_____

_____

_____

_____

_____

_____

_____

_____

The Mission: Today, practice living in the power of the Mattan, moving in the Spirit, becoming more beautiful, strong, and ready for your Wedding Day.

Genesis 34:12; Luke 11:13; Acts 2:1–4; 2 Corinthians 1:22; 5:5

THE HOUSE OF THE DISPOSSESSED

_____

_____

_____

_____

_____

_____

_____

_____

_____

_____

_____

_____

The Mission: Seek, today, to dwell all the more in God's perfect will, that from which you cannot be dispossessed. And pray for the children of Israel.

Deuteronomy 28:30; Luke 13:34–35; 2 Corinthians 5:1

The Anguish of the Jews

THE MYSTERY OF KHAVAH

_____

_____

_____

_____

_____

_____

_____

_____

_____

_____

_____

_____

_____

The Mission: Live today as Khavah, as the helpmate of God to accomplish His purposes on earth—and as the one who bears the life of God into the world.

Genesis 2:18–24; Ephesians 5:31–32

The Khavah Mystery of Existence

THE MOMENTUM KEY

_____

_____

_____

_____

_____

_____

_____

_____

_____

_____

_____

_____

The Mission: Today, apply the momentum key. Avoid wavering. Avoid stopping. Move in consistent godly motion—and to the breakthrough.

1 Corinthians 9:24–27; Philippians 3:13–14; Hebrews 12:1–2

The Momentum Secret

JACOB'S PARADOX

The Mission: Today, come to God as you are, with no covering or pretense, confess what you must confess. Then receive your blessing.

Genesis 27:18–19; 32:27–28; Psalm 32:1–6; Hebrews 4:16; James 4:8

THE BRIT HADDASHAH

_____

_____

_____

_____

_____

_____

_____

_____

_____

_____

_____

The Mission: Come back to the haddashah. Receive anew the love, the grace, the truth, and the salvation that is always new—and be made new.

Jeremiah 31:31–32; Ephesians 4:24; Revelation 21:5

The Brit Haddashah

HEAVEN'S COOKING POTS

The Mission: Live this day as if you were in the kingdom. Let every act be a holy act, sacred in the presence and glory of God.

Zechariah 14:20–21; Colossians 3:23–24

Holy Bells

TAMIM: THE UNBLEMISHED

_____

_____

_____

_____

_____

_____

_____

_____

_____

_____

_____

_____

_____

The Mission: Today, apply the power of tamim to every defilement in your life, past or present. Be complete, spotless, and tamim—just as He is tamim.

Exodus 12:5; 1 Corinthians 5:7; Ephesians 5:27

THE BRIDE AND GROOM PROCESSION

_____

_____

_____

_____

_____

_____

_____

_____

_____

_____

_____

_____

The Mission: This world is only the first house. It is destined to fade away with all its issues and concerns. Live this day in light of that reality.

Jeremiah 33:11; Matthew 25:6; John 14:2–3;
Revelation 19:6–9; 21:1–2

The Blessing of the Bridegroom

THE WAY TO THE MOUNTAINTOP

_____

_____

_____

_____

_____

_____

_____

_____

_____

_____

_____

_____

The Mission: Today, focus only on one course, one path, one journey, one destination, and one direction—up. Aim to go higher with every step.

Psalms 24:3–6; 122; Proverbs 3:6; Philippians 3:14

Secrets of the Mountaintop Walker

SUNERGOS

_____

_____

_____

_____

_____

_____

_____

_____

_____

_____

_____

The Mission: Today, discover and practice the sunergos, the synergy of God. Move in His moving, act in His acting, and live in His living—as one.

1 Corinthians 3:9; Ephesians 6:10; 1 John 4:9

The Two Shall Be One

THE SOLDIERS OF DARKNESS AND LIGHT

_____

_____

_____

_____

_____

_____

_____

_____

_____

_____

_____

_____

_____

_____

_____

_____

The Mission: Give thanks today for all your blessings, and for all your blessings in disguise—those of the past and the still-disguised blessings of the present.

Jeremiah 29:11; Romans 8:28

All Things

THE ROSH PINAH

_____

_____

_____

_____

_____

_____

_____

_____

_____

_____

_____

_____

The Mission: Whatever is incomplete in your life and must be completed, and whatever must be ended, finish it, cap it, with the power of the Capstone.

Psalm 118:22–23; John 19:28–30

The Rosh Pinah

KHATAAH: THE NAME ON YOUR SIN

_____

_____

_____

_____

_____

_____

_____

_____

_____

_____

_____

_____

The Mission: Take every sin, guilt, shame, failure, regret, and mistake in your life, and put His name on each one. Then give to Him that which is His.

Matthew 1:21; 2 Corinthians 5:21

The Sacrifice Mysteries I–V

SECRET OF THE GROGGER

———————————————————

———————————————————

———————————————————

———————————————————

———————————————————

———————————————————

———————————————————

———————————————————

———————————————————

———————————————————

———————————————————

———————————————————

———————————————————

The Mission: What problem, evil, or wrong are you dealing with? Don't dwell on it. Don't react. Dwell on its opposite. Overcome the dark with the light.

Joshua 6:5; Psalm 95:1–2; Matthew 5:44; Romans 12:21

The Grogger

THE VALLEY OF HINNOM

_____

_____

_____

_____

_____

_____

_____

_____

_____

_____

_____

_____

_____

The Mission: Take part in undoing the power of hell. Share the love of God and His salvation with someone who needs to be saved.

Jeremiah 19:1–3; John 3:16; 2 Peter 3:9

The Harvest of Heaven and Hell

BLUEPRINTS OF THE SPIRIT

_____

_____

_____

_____

_____

_____

_____

_____

_____

_____

_____

_____

The Mission: Seek to live this day in the heavenly pattern. Walk, speak, and move by the impulse and leading of the Spirit into the divine blueprint.

Exodus 25:40; 31:2–5; Ezekiel 36:27; Ephesians 2:10;
Hebrews 13:21

Tablets of the Spirit

THE MISHKAN

_____

_____

_____

_____

_____

_____

_____

_____

_____

_____

_____

_____

The Mission: Today, seek to practice the secret of shakan, to dwell in His dwelling, to remain in His remaining, and to abide in His inhabitation.

Exodus 33:9–10; Psalms 16:11; 61:4

Into the Tent of Glory

THE PASSOVER DIP

_____

_____

_____

_____

_____

_____

_____

_____

_____

_____

_____

The Mission: Ponder the love that takes all your sorrows, sufferings, and judgment upon Himself. Live, accordingly, a life worthy of that love.

Exodus 12:8; Matthew 26:20–25; Isaiah 53:4

Passover Seder

THE PROPHECY BOY

_____

_____

_____

_____

_____

_____

_____

_____

_____

_____

_____

_____

The Mission: What do you need to lift up to God? Lift it up—even if it's impossible. Lift up even the course of nations and history.

Daniel 9:1–25; James 5:16; 1 John 5:14

The Resurrection of Zion

THE DIVINE LAW OF ADJECTIVES

_____

_____

_____

_____

_____

_____

_____

_____

_____

_____

_____

_____

_____

The Mission: Today, apply the divine law of adjectives to others and to yourself, see first the noun God created, then give to Him the adjective.

Luke 13:11–16; Acts 9:11–15; 1 Corinthians 6:11

THE REBEGOTTEN

_____

_____

_____

_____

_____

_____

_____

_____

_____

_____

_____

_____

_____

The Mission: As God took on your nature and life, so today, take on His nature, live His life, and walk in the footsteps of the heavenly.

1 Corinthians 15:48–49; Colossians 3:9–10; 1 Peter 1:23

ALTARS ON THE HIGH PLACES

_____

_____

_____

_____

_____

_____

_____

_____

_____

_____

_____

The Mission: Are there any idols or gods in your life, anything you're following above God? Smash the altars of those gods. And live free, wholly to Him who gave Himself wholly to you.

Jeremiah 32:35; Romans 12:1; Ephesians 5:2

HEAVEN'S LOOM

_____

_____

_____

_____

_____

_____

_____

_____

_____

_____

_____

_____

_____

The Mission: Consider how God has woven the threads of your life together for good. Take confidence that with the present threads, He will do the same.

Jeremiah 29:11; Ephesians 1:4; 2 Timothy 1:9

I Know the Plans

THE MYSTERY OF THE GOEL

_____

_____

_____

_____

_____

_____

_____

_____

_____

_____

_____

_____

The Mission: What in your life has never borne the promise and purpose you were meant to bear? Give it to God today. Let Him become your Goel.

Ruth 3:9; Psalm 103:4; Isaiah 54:5

The Goel Redemption

THE WAY OF BREADLESSNESS

_____

_____

_____

_____

_____

_____

_____

_____

_____

_____

_____

_____

_____

The Mission: Practice the state of breadlessness. Empty yourself of all possessions—even the most basic of things—and receive it all anew as a gift from God.

Deuteronomy 8:3; Joshua 13:33; Matthew 6:9–11

THE SPECTRAL MESSIAHS

_____

_____

_____

_____

_____

_____

_____

_____

_____

_____

_____

The Mission: Messiah is the light in which all the colors of the spectrum become one. Bring everything in your life into Him—and it will become light.

Psalm 2; Luke 24:26–27; Revelation 5:11–12

The Rabbinic Mysteries I–VI

THE DOUBLE CALENDAR PARADOX

_____

_____

_____

_____

_____

_____

_____

_____

_____

_____

_____

_____

_____

The Mission: Live this day, not by the old calendar and not according to the old course, but by the calendar in which every day and every moment is new.

Isaiah 43:18–19; John 3:1–8; Colossians 3:5–10

The Mixed Up New Year

THE ANATOLAY MAN

The Mission: Let the light of Messiah shine brighter in your life today. Believe the Sunrise. Live in the power of the Sunrise. Begin today.

Zechariah 3:8; Luke 1:78; 2 Peter 3:18; Revelation 21:23

The Dayspring

THE MYSTERY OF ASENATH

_____

_____

_____

_____

_____

_____

_____

_____

_____

_____

_____

_____

_____

The Mission: Ponder the grace that brought you from far away into the kingdom of Israel. And help bring near those still far away.

Genesis 41:45; Galatians 3:14; Ephesians 2:12, 19

The Shadow Man I–VI

THE STRANGER AT THE WELL

_____

_____

_____

_____

_____

_____

_____

_____

_____

_____

_____

_____

The Mission: Take every need, want, emptiness, desire, or longing and direct it away from the world, to the Spirit and the heavenly.

Genesis 24:11–28; Isaiah 12:3; 55:1; John 4:7–14

The Isaac Rebekah Wedding Mystery I–III

THE MIRACLE WORLD

_____

_____

_____

_____

_____

_____

_____

_____

_____

_____

_____

_____

_____

The Mission: Today, live as if you were in a "miracle world," as if everything you see and hear is miraculous—because it is. Live in the miraculous.

Psalms 8; 19:1–6; Isaiah 6:3

The Miracle World

THE MYSTERY OF THE WOLF

_____

_____

_____

_____

_____

_____

_____

_____

_____

_____

_____

_____

_____

The Mission: Today, stay as far away from temptation as you can, and as close as you can to the Lord. Far from the wolf and near to the Shepherd.

Psalm 23; Ezekiel 34:6–8; Matthew 10:16; John 10:11–14

REBUILDING THE RUINS

_____

_____

_____

_____

_____

_____

_____

_____

_____

_____

_____

_____

_____

The Mission: Is there something broken that you've abandoned or given up on? Pray for its redemption and, if you can, put it back together in God's love.

Isaiah 61:4; Amos 9:14; Luke 4:18; Acts 15:16–17

Dry Bones Rising

DODI LI

_____

_____

_____

_____

_____

_____

_____

_____

_____

_____

_____

_____

The Mission: Make today a Dodi Li day. Live as if God belonged to you—as He does. Receive His life as your gift. And make your life His gift.

Song of Solomon 2:16; Titus 2:14; 1 John 4:10–19

Dodi Li

THE MASTERWORK

The Mission: Today, instead of focusing on the works of God, seek to live in the heart and Spirit of God—and you will accomplish the works of God.

Ezekiel 36:27; Galatians 5:16, 22–25; Philippians 1:6;
Hebrews 13:21

The Poem of God

THE ZYGOTE MYSTERY

_____

_____

_____

_____

_____

_____

_____

_____

_____

_____

The Mission: Learn the secret of the zygote. Let the old self die, crucify the flesh, surrender your will. And the power of life will be released.

Matthew 10:39; John 12:23–24; 15:13; 2 Corinthians 4:10–11

The Mystery of the Zygote

PRUNE THYSELF

_____

_____

_____

_____

_____

_____

_____

_____

_____

_____

_____

_____

The Mission: Today, identify in your life the dead branches, the diseased, the hindering, the wasteful, and the low—and cut them off. Prune thyself.

Mark 1:35; 10:29–30; John 15:1–5

The Secrets of Pruning I–III

THE POWER OF AS

The Mission: Live now not according to who you are but as you are to be. Live this day in the power of *as*—as a victorious, mighty champion!

Judges 6:11–12; Ephesians 5:1, 21–29

The Perfect Bowler

THE YAD

_____

_____

_____

_____

_____

_____

_____

_____

_____

_____

_____

_____

The Mission: Live this day giving thanks and worship at all times, no matter what. Open your life to blessings through the power of the yad.

Psalms 63:4–7; 150; Ephesians 1:12

The Yad People

THE ALPHA COMMANDMENT

_____

_____

_____

_____

_____

_____

_____

_____

_____

_____

_____

_____

_____

The Mission: Is there something in your life that God has called you to do, that you haven't yet done? Open up the blessing. Do it today.

Exodus 12:3; Matthew 23:39; John 1:12; Colossians 2:6–7

The Nisan Lamb

THE GRAPES OF HEAVEN

_____

_____

_____

_____

_____

_____

_____

_____

_____

_____

_____

_____

The Mission: Gather the clusters of the Promised Land—every answered prayer and blessing from God. Take strength from the grapes of heaven and take new ground for God.

Numbers 13:23–28; Romans 8:23; Hebrews 11:1

Clusters of Your Promised Land

THE FEAST OF TRUMPETS

_____

_____

_____

_____

_____

_____

_____

_____

_____

_____

_____

_____

The Mission: Live this day in confidence and hope, looking to the future, knowing He is already there, Lord of the future, and awaiting you to arrive.

Leviticus 23:24; Matthew 24:31; 1 Corinthians 15:52;
1 Thessalonians 4:16

Yom Teruah

THE WARS OF THE HOLY

_____

_____

_____

_____

_____

_____

_____

_____

_____

_____

_____

_____

The Mission: Don't fear the battles. Embrace them. What is of God will be opposed. And that which is good is worth fighting for. Fight the good fight. And you will prevail.

Isaiah 52:1–2; 2 Corinthians 6:4–10; 10:3–5

Jerusalem Besieged

THE SECRET OF THE THIRD PRINCE

_____

_____

_____

_____

_____

_____

_____

_____

_____

_____

_____

_____

The Mission: Practice today the secret of the third prince. In all things, in all situations, fix your eyes on your goal, on Him, and draw continually closer.

Psalm 25:15; Jeremiah 31:9; Hebrews 12:1–2

To Finish the Race

THE DAYS OF TESHUVAH

_____

_____

_____

_____

_____

_____

_____

_____

_____

_____

_____

_____

_____

The Mission: Repentance is an entire life. Live your life in the days of teshuvah. The greater your repentance, the greater will be your return.

Isaiah 30:15; Jeremiah 3:22; Hosea 3:4–5

The Three End-Time Teshuvahs

THE HEAVEN SCENARIO

_____

_____

_____

_____

_____

_____

_____

_____

_____

_____

_____

_____

The Mission: Take your fear, your worry, your anxiety to its end—heaven. And with heaven as your worst scenario, overcome to a fear-free life.

1 Corinthians 2:9; Philippians 1:21–23; Colossians 1:5; 2 Timothy 4:6–8

FIRSTFRUITFULNESS

_____

_____

_____

_____

_____

_____

_____

_____

_____

_____

_____

_____

_____

The Mission: Today, be not only fruitful, but be firstfruitful. Where there is no fruit of love, or hope, forgiveness, or joy, be the first one to bear them.

2 Chronicles 31:5; Matthew 5:44; 1 Corinthians 15:20

The Power of the Bikoreem

THE DEATH OF THE ZACHAR

_____

_____

_____

_____

_____

_____

_____

_____

_____

_____

_____

_____

The Mission: Take all your sins and all that haunts you and cast it onto the Zachar. Reckon it dead in His death. Do likewise with the sins of others.

Exodus 12:3; Jeremiah 31:31–34; 1 Corinthians 5:7;
Hebrews 10:14–17

The Nisan Lamb

THE PRIEST KING

_____

_____

_____

_____

_____

_____

_____

_____

_____

_____

_____

_____

The Mission: The Judge of all has become your Defense Attorney. Therefore, start living today a judgment- and condemnation-free life.

Psalm 110:4; Zechariah 6:12–13; Romans 8:31–34

The Priest King

THE APOSTASIA

_____

_____

_____

_____

_____

_____

_____

_____

_____

_____

_____

The Mission: Take a command from the New Testament and fully carry it out today. Commit to live your life all the more by the Word of God.

Ephesians 6:13; Philippians 2:15; 2 Thessalonians 2:3;
2 Timothy 3:1–4

The Stasis

THE YOM

_____

_____

_____

_____

_____

_____

_____

_____

_____

_____

_____

_____

The Mission: No one knows when they will pass beyond the final veil. Live this day as if it were your last. What must you do?

Romans 14:11–12; 2 Corinthians 5:10, 20–6:2; 1 John 4:17–18

The Mystery of the Three Yom Kippurs

THE SECRET OF THE DESMIOS

_____

_____

_____

_____

_____

_____

_____

_____

_____

_____

_____

_____

The Mission: Nothing can stop the one who walks fully in the will of God. Be that person and break every chain and obstacle to the contrary.

Ephesians 3:1; 4:1; 6:19; Philippians 4:13; 2 Timothy 2:9

Ambassador in Chains

THE TZIPPARIM: THE MYSTERY OF THE BIRDS

_____

_____

_____

_____

_____

_____

_____

_____

_____

_____

_____

_____

_____

_____

_____

_____

The Mission: Immerse every part of your life in Him. Then walk in the power of freedom, cleansing, restoration, and the breaking of curses.

Leviticus 14:1–9; Matthew 8:1–3; Romans 6:3–4; 1 John 1:7

The Mystery of the Tzipparim

THE STATE OF THROUGHNESS

_____

_____

_____

_____

_____

_____

_____

_____

_____

_____

_____

_____

The Mission: Live today in the state of throughness. Make Him your Alpha, the reason for everything you do, and your Omega, the One for whom you live.

2 Corinthians 4:7; 2 Timothy 2:21; Revelation 1:8

The Omega Stone

LORD OF THE TWO VANISHING POINTS

_____

_____

_____

_____

_____

_____

_____

_____

_____

_____

_____

_____

_____

_____

The Mission: Ponder the length of God, the breadth of your salvation, and the love God has for you that spans from everlasting to everlasting.

Psalms 103:12; 113:3; Ephesians 3:18–19; 1 John 1:9

THE PRICE OF THE PRICELESS

_____

_____

_____

_____

_____

_____

_____

_____

_____

_____

_____

The Mission: In view of the treasure freely given, pay the price of the priceless. Give all you have and are. Live all-out. Apprehend the field.

Matthew 13:44; Luke 18:22; Philippians 3:7–8; 2 Peter 1:4

CAMPING IN HEAVEN

_____

_____

_____

_____

_____

_____

_____

_____

_____

_____

_____

_____

The Mission: Learn the secret, while living in the earthly realm, to dwell in the heavenly realm. Live in the realm of heaven and earth as one.

Leviticus 23:40–43; Ephesians 2:6; Revelation 7:9

THE SHEPHERD AND THE FISHERMEN

The Mission: Look back at your life. What is it that you were meant to do and be? Take steps today to all the more fulfill your calling.

Exodus 3:1–8; Jeremiah 1:5; Matthew 4:18–20; Galatians 1:15;
2 Timothy 1:9

The Heavenly Pattern I–IV

ALTAR OF THE HEAVENLIES

_____

_____

_____

_____

_____

_____

_____

_____

_____

_____

_____

_____

_____

The Mission: Bring your life totally inside the cross. It is a doorway. Use its access to go where you never could before.

Exodus 40:6; Leviticus 16:12–14; Hebrews 4:14–16; 10:19–23

THE MYSTERY OF AUTUMN

_____

_____

_____

_____

_____

_____

_____

_____

_____

_____

_____

The Mission: Dwell on the Lion of Judah, the coming King. Live in the power of the Almighty, strong in that which is good, and bold as the Lion.

Daniel 7:13–14; Matthew 24:14; Revelation 11:5; 14:15; 19:16

The Holy Day Finale

THE TENTH OF AV REDEMPTION

_____

_____

_____

_____

_____

_____

_____

_____

_____

_____

_____

_____

_____

The Mission: Remember the Tenth of Av times of your life, how God turned your sorrows into blessing. And know that for every Ninth of Av in your life, God will always give you a Tenth.

Psalm 126; Jeremiah 31:1–16; Joel 2:25; Revelation 7:16–17

The Ninth of Av Mystery

INTO THE GARDEN

_____

_____

_____

_____

_____

_____

_____

_____

_____

_____

_____

_____

The Mission: It is the way of the sacrifice and dying to self that leads into the garden. Choose to walk in that way and enter the blessings of the garden.

Genesis 2:15; Song of Solomon 6:2; Luke 23:43; John 19:41–42

THE END OF THE SCROLL

_____

_____

_____

_____

_____

_____

_____

_____

_____

_____

_____

_____

The Mission: What is it in your life that you must bring to an end in order to enter the new that God has for you? Roll up the scroll today.

Deuteronomy 34; Isaiah 34:4; Revelation 6:14; 20:11; 22

The Alpha and Omega Scroll

THE CHILDREN OF LEAH

_____

_____

_____

_____

_____

_____

_____

_____

_____

_____

_____

_____

The Mission: Commit any sorrow, rejection, frustration, or broken dream into His hands. Believe Him to bring out of it the blessings of Leah.

Genesis 29:31–35; Isaiah 54:1, 4–8; Revelation 5:5

THE LAW OF CHANGE

_____

_____

_____

_____

_____

_____

_____

_____

_____

_____

_____

_____

_____

_____

_____

_____

The Mission: What is the change, the new course God is calling for your life? Focus your energy into the first step and apply the law of new momentum.

Exodus 3:5; Mark 1:17–20; Mark 2:11–12

Spiritual Gear Shifting & the Secret of True Change

THE TISHRI REVELATION

_____

_____

_____

_____

_____

_____

_____

_____

_____

_____

_____

_____

The Mission: In the end, we will appear in the light of God with nothing hidden. Prepare for that day. Remove all darkness. Live now in total light.

Leviticus 23:23–44; Revelation 8:2; 14:7; 19:16; 20:4; 21:3; 22:5

The Lion of Tishri

THE PARADOX SIGN

_____

_____

_____

_____

_____

_____

_____

_____

_____

_____

_____

The Mission: Apply today this most radical power to turn darkness into light, defeat into victory, and death to life. Start turning things upside down.

Isaiah 52:13–15; John 3:14; 1 Corinthians 1:18–28;
Ephesians 1:6–7

The Radical Love

THE DAYS OF ONE-ETERNITIETH

_____

_____

_____

_____

_____

_____

_____

_____

_____

_____

_____

_____

The Mission: Whatever good you would do, do it now. Treat this day as if it comes around only once in an eternity—because it does.

Psalm 90:10–12; Romans 13:11–14; 2 Corinthians 6:1–2; Ephesians 5:16

I Shall Not Pass This Way Again

THE PURPLE MYSTERY

_____

_____

_____

_____

_____

_____

_____

_____

_____

_____

_____

_____

The Mission: Today, join all that is red to all that is blue. Join all that is ungodly to God and God to the ungodly—so much so, it becomes purple.

Exodus 26:31; John 19:1–6; Philippians 4:5–7; 1 Timothy 1:15

The Purple Mystery I–IV

THE SABBATH OF AGES

_____

_____

_____

_____

_____

_____

_____

_____

_____

_____

_____

_____

The Mission: Make the Lord of the Sabbath all the more the Lord of your life. And learn the secret of dwelling in the Sabbath age even now.

Exodus 20:8–11; Isaiah 11:1–9; Mark 2:27–28

The Age of Shabbat

THE DAY OF TIME AND TIMELESSNESS

_____

_____

_____

_____

_____

_____

_____

_____

_____

_____

_____

_____

_____

The Mission: Your future is already contained by your salvation and covered by it. Ponder this fact and, by it, be at peace and live in confidence.

Isaiah 1:18; 53; 1 John 1:7; Revelation 13:8

Divine Hebrew Time Travel

THE PROMISED LAND WILDERNESS

_____

_____

_____

_____

_____

_____

_____

_____

_____

_____

_____

_____

The Mission: Heaven is not only after this life, but within it. Live this day as the commencement of heavenly life, the beginning of heaven.

Isaiah 35:1–10; 40:3–4; 51:3; Hebrews 11:9–10

The Midbar

THE RUSSIAN CASE

_____

_____

_____

_____

_____

_____

_____

_____

_____

_____

_____

_____

The Mission: Ponder this fact: the Word of God is stronger than powers, even superpowers. Today, live accordingly, and use that power for victory.

Genesis 12:3; Deuteronomy 7:9; Jeremiah 16:15

The Chaldean Secret of World History I–III

THE X OF THE MIRACLE

_____

_____

_____

_____

_____

_____

_____

_____

_____

_____

_____

_____

_____

_____

The Mission: Apply today the power of *X*. Do what you could not have done and live what you could not have lived except by the power of *X*.

Acts 4:7–33; Romans 8:10–15; 1 Corinthians 15:3–8; 1 John 1:1–4

The Resurrection Factor

THE SECRET NAME OF GOD

_____

_____

_____

_____

_____

_____

_____

_____

_____

_____

_____

_____

_____

The Mission: Speak God's secret name—the God of you, the God of your name. Ponder what that means: He's the God of all you are and has chosen your name in His.

Genesis 32:29–33:20; Psalm 18:2; Isaiah 48:1

Yeshuati

THE ISHMAEL MYSTERY

The Mission: Live today not focusing on the blessings you don't have, but dwelling on all the blessings you do.

Genesis 17:20–21; 21:12–21; Ephesians 4:30–5:21

THE SEASONS OF THE HARVEST

_____

_____

_____

_____

_____

_____

_____

_____

_____

_____

_____

_____

_____

The Mission: Today is the day of the harvest. Share the good news. Show your love. Forgive. Bless. Don't wait. The time of your harvest is only now.

Ecclesiastes 3:1; Jeremiah 8:20; Matthew 9:37; Luke 10:2

Seasons of the Harvest

THE FACES OF GOD

_____

_____

_____

_____

_____

_____

_____

_____

_____

_____

_____

_____

The Mission: Today make it your aim to see the faces of God in all their appearances. And be one of them.

Genesis 32:30; Numbers 6:24–27; Matthew 5:8;
2 Corinthians 3:7, 13, 18

The Face of Messiah

BAAL ZEVUV

_____

_____

_____

_____

_____

_____

_____

_____

_____

_____

_____

_____

The Mission: Is there anything you're living for, serving, putting first, above God? See it for what it is—Baal Zevuv. Flee from it today like the devil.

1 Kings 18:21; 1 Thessalonians 1:9; James 4:7;
1 John 2:15–17; 5:21

The God of a Thousand Faces

THE DAY OF NEOGENESIS

_____

_____

_____

_____

_____

_____

_____

_____

_____

_____

_____

_____

_____

The Mission: Where in your life do you need a genesis? Take the power of the resurrection, the Resheet, and declare into your life, "Let there be Light!"

Genesis 1:1–3; Luke 24:4–7; 2 Corinthians 4:6; 5:17

The Genesis Day

LIVING FROM THE FUTURE

_____

_____

_____

_____

_____

_____

_____

_____

_____

_____

_____

_____

The Mission: Learn the secret today of living from the future, fight your won battle, accomplish your done work, and live from the finished you.

Matthew 6:10; 16:18; Mark 11:24; Ephesians 4:1

As It Is in Heaven

THE MYSTERY SCROLL

_____

_____

_____

_____

_____

_____

_____

_____

_____

_____

_____

_____

The Mission: Today, translate the Scripture into thought, action, reality, life. Make your life a scroll, a living translation of the Word of God.

Jeremiah 31:33; Matthew 5:16; 2 Corinthians 3:2–3

THE LOGOS CRUCIFIED

_____

_____

_____

_____

_____

_____

_____

_____

_____

_____

_____

_____

_____

The Mission: The Logos has died, and with it, your old life. So stop letting the past affect you. Live free today in the newness of having no past.

Isaiah 43:18–19; 44:22–23; John 1:1–14; 2 Corinthians 5:14–17; Revelation 21:1–5

The Keburah

THE POWER OF APOLUO

_____

_____

_____

_____

_____

_____

_____

_____

_____

_____

_____

_____

The Mission: Today, apply the power of apoluo. Release and you shall be released, loosed, freed, made whole, and sent forth.

Leviticus 25:10; Matthew 27:26; Luke 6:37; 13:12; Galatians 5:1

UNDER THE HUPPAH

_____

_____

_____

_____

_____

_____

_____

_____

_____

_____

_____

_____

_____

The Mission: Spread today God's huppah over your life. Bring every part of your life under His covering and pronounce it "married."

Psalm 91:1–4; Song of Solomon 2:3–4; Isaiah 4:2–6

Under the Huppah

ADONAI

_____

_____

_____

_____

_____

_____

_____

_____

_____

_____

_____

_____

_____

The Mission: Ponder and live the mystery of Adonai, make the Lord your "my Lord" whom you follow and submit to with endless exclamation points.

Ezekiel 36:22–23; Daniel 9:4; Zechariah 13:9; John 20:28

YHVH

THE CHILDREN OF THE EIGHTH DAY

_____

_____

_____

_____

_____

_____

_____

_____

_____

_____

_____

_____

_____

The Mission: Learn the secret of living in the Eighth Day—beyond the flesh, beyond the world, beyond the self, beyond the old—in the beyond of now.

John 20:1; Acts 20:7; Romans 6:5–11; 12:2; 1 John 4:4

The Mystery of the Eighth Day I–III

AWAKE THE DAWN

_____

_____

_____

_____

_____

_____

_____

_____

_____

_____

_____

The Mission: Today, turn your eyes away from darkness. Turn them back to the Light. Cause the sun to rise. Awake the dawn!

Psalms 57:8; 112:4; Acts 26:18; Romans 13:12

She Like the Dawn

THE CENTRALITY FACTOR

_____

_____

_____

_____

_____

_____

_____

_____

_____

_____

_____

_____

The Mission: Whatever is of God is in the center. Put the things of God in the center of this day. And make God the center around which your life revolves.

Deuteronomy 4:34–35; 32:8; Zechariah 8:23; Isaiah 2:3

THE JOSIAH PRINCIPLE

_____

_____

_____

_____

_____

_____

_____

_____

_____

_____

_____

_____

The Mission: Take God's Word today and obey it. By obeying the revealed will of God, you will be led into the unrevealed will of God—your destiny.

2 Kings 23:15–17; Psalm 37:23; Proverbs 2:20–21; 3:5–6;
Ephesians 2:10

Entering Your Prophetic Destiny

THE NIGHT CANDLE

_____

_____

_____

_____

_____

_____

_____

_____

_____

_____

_____

_____

The Mission: Live today as a candle in the night. Don't fear the darkness or be intimidated by it. But shine all the more brightly against the night.

Matthew 5:14–16; 13:43; John 1:5; Philippians 2:15; 1 Peter 4:14

THE I AM REDEMPTION

_____

_____

_____

_____

_____

_____

_____

_____

_____

_____

_____

The Mission: Let your fallen I Am be finished in His death and let His risen and victorious I Am become the I am of your life.

Exodus 3:14; John 8:58; Colossians 2:9–12

The I Am Revelation

MOUNTAINS AND CAPSTONES

_____

_____

_____

_____

_____

_____

_____

_____

_____

_____

_____

_____

The Mission: Today, see every problem, obstacle, trouble, and adversity as a mountain to be turned into a capstone. Take part in turning it.

Genesis 50:15–21; Isaiah 60; Zechariah 4:6–9; James 1:2–4

Mountains and Capstones

THE GLORY INSIDE THE TENT

_____

_____

_____

_____

_____

_____

_____

_____

_____

_____

_____

_____

_____

The Mission: Go beyond the curtains today, deeper and deeper into the tent of meeting to the innermost sanctum, until you find His glory.

Exodus 40:34–36; Psalm 27:4; Ezekiel 44:16; Hebrews 4:16

THE SECRET HEBREW PROPHECIES

_____

_____

_____

_____

_____

_____

_____

_____

_____

_____

_____

_____

_____

_____

The Mission: Live today as if your life was a prophecy, existing solely to be fulfilled by His presence and, in that fulfilling, to glorify Him.

Philippians 1:6; Colossians 2:9–10; 1 Thessalonians 5:24;
2 Thessalonians 1:11

Finding Your Destiny

YOUR PRESENT AFTERLIFE

_____

_____

_____

_____

_____

_____

_____

_____

_____

_____

_____

The Mission: Today, live as if your life was over. Then enter your afterlife, beyond the flesh and the earthly, to live in the Spirit, in the heavenly.

Romans 6:4–11; 8:10–14; Galatians 2:20; Colossians 3:1–9

How to Enter Your Afterlife Now

THE GUARDIAN

_____

_____

_____

_____

_____

_____

_____

_____

_____

_____

_____

_____

_____

_____

The Mission: Live today in the leading of the Spirit. Go only where He goes. Move as He moves. Let your every step be guided by His.

Genesis 24:51–61; John 16:13; Romans 8:14

The Isaac Rebekah Wedding Mystery I–III

THE MOSES PARADIGM

_____

_____

_____

_____

_____

_____

_____

_____

_____

_____

_____

_____

The Mission: How has God saved you, loved you, and touched your life? Use your life to do the same for others. Begin today.

Exodus 2:1–10; Matthew 10:8; John 15:9; Ephesians 3:7–8

Graduation I–II

THE MYSTERY OF MELCHIZEDEK

_____

_____

_____

_____

_____

_____

_____

_____

_____

_____

_____

_____

_____

The Mission: Those who are of the Melchi-Zedek, Messiah, the Royal Priest, are royal priests. Learn today what that means and live as one, in righteousness, holiness, royalty, and power.

Genesis 14:18–20; Psalm 110; Isaiah 53:11; Hebrews 7:1–21

THE KARAT

_____

_____

_____

_____

_____

_____

_____

_____

_____

_____

_____

_____

The Mission: The karat is the sign and assurance that your sins are absolutely remembered no more. Live in the confidence and repercussions of that fact.

Jeremiah 31:31–34; Daniel 9:24–26; Hebrews 9:14; 13:20–21

A Most Holy Verse

THE NAME IN WHICH YOU ARE

_____

_____

_____

_____

_____

_____

_____

_____

_____

_____

_____

_____

_____

The Mission: Ponder this mystery: You are in His Name. He was named for you. You are joined forever. Seek what that means. And live this day in that joining.

Isaiah 12:1–3; Jeremiah 23:5–7; 33:16; Matthew 1:21; John 1:1–2

Yeshuati

THE SCEPTER OF JUDAH

The Mission: Even the Book of Sanhedrin bears witness that Messiah has come. Live this day and beyond a life that manifests that fact.

Genesis 49:10; Matthew 26:63–64; Ephesians 1:20–22; Colossians 15:24–28

The Scepter of Judah

THE GARDEN OF MIRACLES

_____

_____

_____

_____

_____

_____

_____

_____

_____

_____

_____

_____

The Mission: Take all in your life that failed, that was taken or lost, that was broken, or that came to an end, all your sorrows. Come to the Tomb and plant them in the Garden of Miracles.

Genesis 1:27–29; Isaiah 61:3; John 19:31–20:16;
1 Corinthians 15:36–37, 42–44

The Gardener

THE RETURN OF THE PROTOTYPE

_____

_____

_____

_____

_____

_____

_____

_____

_____

_____

_____

The Mission: Divest yourself today from worldly attachments, that you might gain spiritual power. Exchange a comfortable walk for a revolutionary one.

Zechariah 8:3–8; Matthew 23:37–39; Acts 2:16–18, 39; Romans 11

The Mystery of the Rains

DOWN THE MOUNTAIN

_____

_____

_____

_____

_____

_____

_____

_____

_____

_____

_____

_____

_____

_____

_____

The Mission: Dwell today on the mountaintop with God. Receive His blessings. Then bring them down the mountain to touch your world.

Exodus 34:28–31; Psalm 96:1–3; Isaiah 58:5–11; Acts 1:8

THE UNCAUSED CAUSE

_____

_____

_____

_____

_____

_____

_____

_____

_____

_____

_____

_____

_____

The Mission: Today, make it your aim to receive the love of God with no reason or cause. And love others the same way, with no reason or cause.

Luke 6:27–36; 23:33–34; 1 Corinthians 13; 1 John 4:7–12

The Unknowable Love

THE SEVEN MYSTERIES OF THE AGE

_____

_____

_____

_____

_____

_____

_____

_____

_____

_____

_____

_____

The Mission: Time is framed by the holy days of God. Live today as a holy day, a sacred day, centered in the presence of God. And it will be so.

Leviticus 23

The Seven Mysteries of the Age I–VII

THE SUNRISE REDEMPTION

_____

_____

_____

_____

_____

_____

_____

_____

_____

_____

_____

The Mission: Believe in God's power to bring into existence that which is not. Live this day in that power. Speak that which is not as if it was.

Isaiah 60:1; Matthew 27:57–60; 28:1–6; Ephesians 5:14;
1 Thessalonians 5:5

PERFORMING YOUR SEMIKHAH

_____

_____

_____

_____

_____

_____

_____

_____

_____

_____

_____

_____

_____

The Mission: Perform the sacred Semikhah. Place your hands on His head. Lay your life upon His life. Release what must be released. And be released.

Leviticus 16:21; Galatians 2:20; 1 Peter 5:7; 1 John 1:8–9

Footsteps on the Altar

HEAVENLY NOSTALGIA

_____

_____

_____

_____

_____

_____

_____

_____

_____

_____

_____

_____

The Mission: Live this day as if your life was over, but you were given a second chance to go back. Do now what, in heaven, you can never do again.

Psalm 90:9–12; John 4:35–36; 1 Thessalonians 5:16–18;
James 1:17

THE JUBILEE MAN

_____

_____

_____

_____

_____

_____

_____

_____

_____

_____

_____

_____

_____

_____

The Mission: If you belong to Messiah, you have the power of Jubilee, the power to restore the lost and the broken. Today, live, speak, and use that power.

Leviticus 25:10–11; Joel 2:25–27; Zechariah 8:7–8; Luke 4:18–19; Acts 1:6

The Prophetic Jubilee

THE FOUR CORNERS OF THE ALTAR

_____

_____

_____

_____

_____

_____

_____

_____

_____

_____

_____

The Mission: Ponder this truth: The love of God is bigger than the universe, stronger than evil, and longer than time. In that, overcome all that you must overcome.

Exodus 40:6; Psalm 118:27; Galatians 6:14; Hebrews 13:10

ENTERING THE HEAVENLY DIMENSION

_____

_____

_____

_____

_____

_____

_____

_____

_____

_____

_____

_____

The Mission: Enter this day beyond the veil, into the deep and deeper and deeper of His presence, to dwell in the dimension of the heavenlies.

Psalm 100; Hebrews 9:3–5; 10:19–20; 2 Corinthians 12:1–4

SPECIFICITY

_____

_____

_____

_____

_____

_____

_____

_____

_____

_____

_____

_____

The Mission: Manifest the love of God in specificity. Bless specific people with specific actions of love—specifically today.

Matthew 25:31–46; Luke 2:1–20; Galatians 4:4–5; 1 John 4:20–21

God With Us

DESERT RAINS

_____

_____

_____

_____

_____

_____

_____

_____

_____

_____

_____

_____

The Mission: Your entire life is as a desert waiting for the desert rains to blossom, to flow, and to produce miracles. Seek today the desert rains.

Isaiah 35:1–2, 6–7; 43:19; 44:3–4

The Arabah

THE CALAH

_____

_____

_____

_____

_____

_____

_____

_____

_____

_____

_____

_____

The Mission: Marry every imperfect part of your life to the Bridegroom. Let Him fill in all that is missing. See yourself in the eyes of His love—as the calah—the perfect one.

Isaiah 62:5; Matthew 5:48; Ephesians 5:25–27; Revelation 19:7–8

The Mystery of the Calah

GOD ON THE BLUE PLANET

_____

_____

_____

_____

_____

_____

_____

_____

_____

_____

_____

The Mission: Make it your aim this day to live the life of God in this world. Live to bless, to fill, to save, to overcome, and to change the world.

John 15:14–16; Ephesians 1:20–21; Colossians 1:10–11; Hebrews 13:8

God on the Blue Planet

THE ATZERET

The Mission: In heaven, the good of this life will be retained. Do not retain anything of this day that is not good. Retain only what is.

Matthew 6:20; 19:21; Revelation 7:9–17; 21:12–14

The Mystery of the Eighth Day I–III

THE INVISIBLE HARP

_____

_____

_____

_____

_____

_____

_____

_____

_____

_____

_____

_____

_____

The Mission: Today, learn to make music from the instrument of your heart—from the deepest part of your being—the melody of praise, joy, and worship.

Psalm 33:1–5; Ephesians 5:19–20

Melody in Your Heart

THE SHABBAT MYSTERY CODE

_____

_____

_____

_____

_____

_____

_____

_____

_____

_____

_____

_____

The Mission: In God, the best comes at the end. Live this day in full confidence of that fact, looking forward, and preparing in hope for that day.

Exodus 31:16–17; Isaiah 2:1–5; 66:22–23; Matthew 12:8

The Shabbat Mystery Code I–II

THE OTHER THROUGH THE ONE

_____

_____

_____

_____

_____

_____

_____

_____

_____

_____

_____

_____

_____

The Mission: Take part in the mystery today. Let the life, the love, the goodness, the power, and the presence of God, through your life, be born.

Genesis 2:21–23; 1 Corinthians 11:11–12; Ephesians 5:25–32

Male and Female

THE RESURRECTION LAND

_____

_____

_____

_____

_____

_____

_____

_____

_____

_____

_____

_____

The Mission: Your life is a resurrection. Follow, in the Word of God, the pattern for life and become the person you were created to become.

Jeremiah 30–31; Hosea 6:2; Amos 9:14–15; Ephesians 2:6

The Resurrection of Zion

THE END OF THE STORY

_____

_____

_____

_____

_____

_____

_____

_____

_____

_____

_____

_____

_____

The Mission: No matter what you're going through today or in your life, believe, look to, and live in confidence to the end of the story.

Job 42:10–17; Luke 24:46–53; 2 Corinthians 2:14; Hebrews 12:1–2

The End of the Story

THE RUNNER'S RIDDLE

The Mission: Commit today that no matter what, even if you fall, you'll keep running until you cross the finish line. And if you've fallen, make today the day you get up and get going.

Proverbs 24:16; 1 Corinthians 9:24; Hebrews 12:1

To Finish the Race

THE MACCABEAN BLUEPRINT

_____

_____

_____

_____

_____

_____

_____

_____

_____

_____

_____

_____

_____

The Mission: Live today by the Maccabean Blueprint. Stand with God and don't be moved. Go against the odds. Fight the fight. Light up the darkness.

Daniel 11:32; Zechariah 9:13–14; Ephesians 6:10–20; Revelation 12:11

The Maccabee Blueprint I–IV

HEAVEN'S WOMB

_____

_____

_____

_____

_____

_____

_____

_____

_____

_____

_____

_____

The Mission: Take part in a new revelation—see everything in your life, as your preparation for eternal life. See this life as the womb of heaven. And live your life accordingly.

Psalm 139:13–16; Matthew 18:3; 19:7; John 16:21–22;
Romans 8:22–23, 29

THE MASK OF THE EGYPTIAN

_____

_____

_____

_____

_____

_____

_____

_____

_____

_____

_____

_____

The Mission: Pray for the peace of Jerusalem and for His ancient people to see through the mask and behold Messiah, their long-lost brother, Yeshua.

Genesis 44:18; 45:1–2; Hosea 3:4–5; Zechariah 12:10–13:1; Matthew 23:37–39

The Shadow Man I–VI

AS A MAN CARRIES HIS SON

_____

_____

_____

_____

_____

_____

_____

_____

_____

_____

_____

_____

The Mission: Thank God for the times in your life when you couldn't go on, but God carried you. Let those same arms carry you and your burdens now.

Deuteronomy 1:31; Song of Solomon 8:5; Isaiah 40:11; 46:3–4;
John 10:27–29

THE IMMANUEL PARADOX

_____

_____

_____

_____

_____

_____

_____

_____

_____

_____

_____

_____

The Mission: Remember those times in your life when you felt farthest from God. Now ponder this: God was there feeling just as far from God with you. So nothing will ever separate you from the love of God.

Isaiah 43:2; Matthew 27:46; 28:19–20; Romans 8:35–39

Immanuel I–II

THE GREAT ASCENDING

_____

_____

_____

_____

_____

_____

_____

_____

_____

_____

_____

_____

The Mission: Take time today to look back at the big picture. See how far God has taken you. Press on in your journey step by step to the heights.

Psalms 18:36; 84:5–7; 122; Isaiah 2:1–2; Philippians 3:13–14

Higher Ground

THE GARDENER

_____

_____

_____

_____

_____

_____

_____

_____

_____

_____

_____

The Mission: Today, let the Gardener come into His garden, to every part of your life, especially the untouched soil, that every part would bear its fruit.

Genesis 1:29; 2:15; Song of Solomon 4:16; 5:1; 6:2; John 20:13–20

THE MISSION PLANET

The Mission: You are already on the mission planet. Start living today not as one at home, but as one sent here on assignment. Fulfill your mission.

John 8:23; 17:16–18; Acts 13:3–5; 2 Corinthians 5:20; Hebrews 3:1

THE ANGELIC MEASURING ROD

_____

_____

_____

_____

_____

_____

_____

_____

_____

_____

_____

_____

_____

_____

The Mission: Take the Word of God today and follow its exact measurements and specifications and you will walk into the exact dimensions of God's will for your life.

Isaiah 46:10–13; Jeremiah 21:11; Ezekiel 40:1–5;
Revelation 11:1; 21:15

The Heavenly Pattern I–IV

THE BOOK OF AGES

_____

_____

_____

_____

_____

_____

_____

_____

_____

_____

_____

_____

_____

The Mission: Don't try to understand your life from the middle. But know that as you follow His leading, your story will, in the end, become perfect.

Genesis 1–3; Hebrews 3:14; 12:2; Revelation 20:1–22:3

The Word

THE BRIDE AND GROOM IN THE MARRIAGE CHAMBER

_____

_____

_____

_____

_____

_____

_____

_____

_____

_____

_____

_____

The Mission: Today, enter into the marital chamber and dwell there with your Beloved, you and God, alone, and nothing else.

Song of Solomon 1:4; 2:14; 1 Corinthians 13:12; Revelation 22:4

Under the Huppah

SHEMEN

_____

_____

_____

_____

_____

_____

_____

_____

_____

_____

_____

_____

The Mission: Discover the mystery of shemen. Live in the power of the Spirit, beyond your limitations, over and above, exceeding, transcending, overflowing, and dwelling in the heavenlies.

Exodus 30:30–31; John 7:37–39; Acts 1:8; Romans 15:19;
Galatians 5:22–25

The Spirit-Filled Life

THE REBEGETTING

_____

_____

_____

_____

_____

_____

_____

_____

_____

_____

_____

_____

_____

The Mission: Life must beget life. Whatever you have received, you must give. Love others, bless others, give to others, and save others— as God has done to you.

Deuteronomy 3:14, 23; 34:9; Matthew 10:5–8; 28:19–20;
John 14:12; 2 Timothy 4:1–2

Graduation I–II

THE PELEH

_____

_____

_____

_____

_____

_____

_____

_____

_____

_____

_____

_____

The Mission: Get back to the Peleh, the wonder of His love, the miracle of your salvation, and the power to do the impossible.

Exodus 15:11; Isaiah 9:6; Acts 2:43; Ephesians 3:19

Peleh

THE SEVEN MYSTERIES OF YOUR LIFE

_____

_____

_____

_____

_____

_____

_____

_____

_____

_____

_____

_____

_____

The Mission: God has ordained appointed times for your life—so too for your days. Seek and find His appointed times and moments of this day.

Leviticus 23; Psalm 139:16

The Moedeem and the Mystery of Your Life

THE LAND OF BEYOND

The Mission: Ponder the day you'll cross over into the Promised Land. And give thanks that He Who will be with you *then*, is with you right *now*.

Deuteronomy 8:7–9; 26:15; Joshua 1:1–4; 1 Peter 1:3–4; Revelation 21:1–4

The Mystery of the Eighth Day I–III

THE MYSTERY OF THE PLURALITIES

_____

_____

_____

_____

_____

_____

_____

_____

_____

_____

_____

_____

The Mission: Take time today to meditate and dwell on where you will dwell forever, and on all its never-ending and everlasting pluralities.

1 Corinthians 2:9; Ephesians 3:20–21; Revelation 22:1–5

The Hebrew Mysteries I–IV

THE TIME OF KNOWING

_____

_____

_____

_____

_____

_____

_____

_____

_____

_____

_____

The Mission: Since it will take an eternity for you to know God, there's so much for you to discover. Seek to know Him today as if for the first time.

Psalms 23:6; 27:4; 63; Matthew 18:3–4; Philippians 3:10

The Mystery of the Eighth Day I–III

THE BLESSING WITH NO END

_____

_____

_____

_____

_____

_____

_____

_____

_____

_____

_____

_____

The Mission: Receive this day the blessing Messiah gave His disciples. It was to you as well. Receive as much as you can. It has no end."

Psalms 21:6; 106; Luke 24:50–53; Revelation 22:21

The Unended

HOME

The Mission: You are not yet home. Live today in light of that. Set your heart away from that which is not home, and toward that which is.

John 17:16; Psalm 46:4–5; Hebrews 13:14; John 14:1–3

The Blessing of the Bridegroom

THE TWO SHALL BE ONE

_____

_____

_____

_____

_____

_____

_____

_____

_____

_____

_____

_____

The Mission: Join every part of your life to His life and let every part of His life be joined to yours. Unlock, experience, and live this mystery—the two shall become one.

Genesis 2:24; 1 Corinthians 6:17; Ephesians 5:31–32;
The Song of Solomon

The Two Shall Be One

TO GO DEEPER, TO FIND MORE, TO CONTINUE THE JOURNEY...

A T THE BOTTOM of every mystery you'll find a title. The title identifies the full teaching or message from Jonathan Cahn that goes deeper into the mystery, or gives more than can be given on one page, or presents a complementary teaching or message that supplements the mystery given.

———•———

To receive these teachings, go to HopeOfTheWorld.org and to the list of all of Jonathan's messages, and search by the title or keyword.

———•———

Or you can write to Hope of the World, Box 1111, Lodi, NJ 07644, USA and request to order them by name.

Jonathan Cahn has been called the prophetic voice of our generation. He caused a stir throughout America and around the world starting with the release of his first book, *The Harbinger,* bringing him to national and international prominence. He's spoken at the United Nations, to Members of Congress on Capitol Hill, and has been interviewed on countless television, radio, and other media programs.

He leads Hope of the World ministries, an international outreach of Jew and Gentile committed to spreading God's Word to the nations and helping the world's most needy. He also leads the Jerusalem Center/Beth Israel, a worship center made up of Jews and Gentiles, people of all backgrounds, just outside New York City, in Wayne, New Jersey. He is a much sought-after speaker and appears throughout America and around the world. He is a Jewish follower of Jesus.

To get in touch with Jonathan Cahn's ministry, to get more and deeper into the mysteries, to receive free gifts, prophetic updates, other teachings, messages, or special communications from Jonathan, or to have a part in spreading God's Word, helping the needy across the world, and have a part in God's end-time work and purposes, here's how:

Write to:
Hope of the World, Box 1111, Lodi, NJ 07644
Or go to: hopeoftheworld.org and
www.facebook.com/Jonathan-Cahn-Official-Site-255143021176055

CONNECT WITH US!

CHARISMA HOUSE
(Spiritual Growth)

Facebook.com/CharismaHouse

@CharismaHouse

Instagram.com/CharismaHouseBooks

SILOAM
(Health)

Pinterest.com/CharismaHouse

REALMS
(Fiction)

Facebook.com/RealmsFiction